走近中国

INTRODUCTION

TO

CHINA

（汉英对照）

李淑霞◎编著

知识产权出版社

全国百佳图书出版单位

图书在版编目（CIP）数据

走近中国：汉英对照 / 李淑霞编著 . —北京：知识产权出版社，2019.6
ISBN 978-7-5130-6259-6

Ⅰ.①走… Ⅱ.①李… Ⅲ.①汉语—对外汉语教学—教材 Ⅳ.① H195.4

中国版本图书馆 CIP 数据核字（2019）第 093766 号

责任编辑：陈晶晶　　　　　　　　　　　　责任校对：谷　洋
封面设计：李志伟　　　　　　　　　　　　责任印制：孙婷婷

走近中国（汉英对照）

Introduction to China

李淑霞　编著

出版发行：**知识产权出版社**有限责任公司	网　　址：http：//www.ipph.cn
社　　址：北京市海淀区气象路 50 号院	邮　　编：100081
责编电话：010-82000860 转 8391	责编邮箱：shiny-chjj@163.com
发行电话：010-82000860 转 8101/8102	发行传真：010-82000893/82005070/82000270
印　　刷：北京建宏印刷有限公司	经　　销：各大网上书店、新华书店及相关专业书店
开　　本：720mm×1000mm　1/16	印　　张：13.5
版　　次：2019 年 6 月第 1 版	印　　次：2019 年 6 月第 1 次印刷
字　　数：240 千字	定　　价：79.00 元

ISBN 978-7-5130-6259-6

Introduction of the Book

Introduction to China is a textbook taking foreign students as the teaching objects. The main purpose of teaching is to give foreign students a general understanding of the basic state of Chinese society. The main teaching contents include the following nine parts: China's territory, China's history, China's population, China's ethnic groups, China's customs, China's arts, China's tourism, China's international contacts and Chinese temperaments.

In view of the limited Chinese reading ability of foreign students, this textbook is presented in both Chinese and English in order that international students can better understand and comprehend the contents of the textbook. At the same time, Chinese-English bilingual reading is also conductive to improving the Chinese reading level of international students.

序 言

　　《走近中国》是以外国留学生为教学对象编写的一部教材，主要教学目的是让外国留学生对中国社会的基本状况有一个大致的了解。主要教学内容包括以下9个部分：中国的国土、中国的历史、中国的人口、中国的民族、中国的习俗、中国的艺术、中国的旅游、中国的国际交往和中国人的气质。

　　鉴于外国留学生的汉语阅读水平有限，这本教材采取了汉英对照的呈现方式，以便留学生能够更好地理解和领会教材内容，同时，汉英双语对照阅读也有利于提高留学生的汉语阅读水平。

　　近年来，我一直从事留学生的"中国概况"课程教学工作，可以说，这本教材是我教学工作实践的积累和结晶，因此，它在很大的程度上具有独特性、主观性和局限性。本书结稿之后，我还将继续从事留学生"中国概况"课程的教学工作，并将继续对教学内容进行更新、补充和完善。

Preface

Introduction to China is a textbook taking foreign students as the teaching objects. The main purpose of teaching is to give foreign students a general understanding of the basic state of Chinese society. The main teaching contents include the following nine parts: China's territory, China's history, China's population, China's ethnic groups, China's customs, China's arts, China's tourism, China's international contacts and Chinese temperaments.

In view of the limited Chinese reading ability of foreign students, this textbook is presented in both Chinese and English in order that international students can better understand and comprehend its contents. At the same time, Chinese-English bilingual reading is also conductive to improving the Chinese reading level of international students.

For the past few years, I have been engaged in the teaching of "Chinese Overview" for foreign students. It can be said that the textbook is the accumulation and crystallization of my teaching practice. Therefore, to a great extent, it has individuality, subjectivity and limitations. After this textbook is finished, I will continue to engage in the teaching work and to update, supplement and perfect the teaching contents.

目 录

第一章　中国的国土 2

  第一节　中国的地理 2

  第二节　中国的气候 12

  第三节　中国的资源 16

  第四节　中国的行政区划 18

第二章　中国的历史 32

  第一节　中国古代史（1840 年以前） 32

  第二节　中国近代史（1840—1919 年） 40

  第三节　中国现代史（1919—1949 年） 46

  第四节　中国当代史（1949 年 10 月至今） 52

第三章　中国的人口 56

  第一节　中国的人口演变 58

  第二节　中国的人口结构 60

  第三节　中国的计划生育政策 60

第四章　中国的民族 64

  第一节　中国的民族状况 66

  第二节　中国的民族政策 68

  第三节　中国少数民族的发展变化 70

Contents

Chapter 1 China's Territory 3

    Section 1 China's Geography 3

    Section 2 China's Climate 13

    Section 3 China's Resources 17

    Section 4 China's Administrative Division 19

Chapter 2 History of China 33

    Section 1 Ancient History of China (Before 1840) 33

    Section 2 Early Modern History of China (1840—1919) 41

    Section 3 Modern History of China (1919—1949) 47

    Section 4 Contemporary History of China (Since 1949,10) 53

Chapter 3 Population of China 57

    Section 1 Population Evolution of China 59

    Section 2 Demographic Structure of China 61

    Section 3 Birth Control Policy of China 61

Chapter 4 Ethnic Groups of China 65

    Section 1 Conditions of China's Minorities 67

    Section 2 The Ethnic Policy of China 69

    Section 3 Developments and Changes of China's Minorities 71

第五章　中国的习俗 72

第一节　中国的婚姻家庭 72

第二节　中国的节庆假日 76

第三节　中国的饭菜酒茶 94

第六章　中国的艺术 102

第一节　中国的书法·绘画 102

第二节　中国的音乐·舞蹈 110

第三节　中国的戏剧·电影 126

第四节　中国的曲艺·杂技 150

第七章　中国的旅游 158

第一节　中国的旅游资源 158

第二节　中国名城选介 164

第八章　中国的国际交往 182

第一节　中国的外交关系 182

第二节　中国的文化交流 184

第三节　"一带一路"——发展倡议 188

第九章　中国人的气质 194

参考文献 204

后记——致谢 206

Chapter 5 China's Customs 73

Section 1 Chinese Marriages and Families 73

Section 2 Chinese Festivals and Holidays 77

Section 3 Chinese Foods Dishes Liquors and Teas 95

Chapter 6 Chinese Arts 103

Section 1 Chinese Calligraphy and Painting 103

Section 2 Chinese Music and Dances 111

Section 3 Chinese Dramas and Movies 127

Section 4 Chinese Qu Yi and Acrobatics 151

Chapter 7 Chinese Tourism 159

Section 1 Chinese Tourism Resources 159

Section 2 Selective Introduction of the Famous Chinese Cities 165

Chapter 8 China's International Contacts 183

Section 1 China's Diplomatic Relations 183

Section 2 China's Cultural Exchanges 185

Section 3 One Belt and One Road—Development Initiative 189

Chapter 9 The Temperaments of the Chinese People 195

Bibliography 204

Postscript–Acknowledgement 206

第一章 中国的国土

中国疆域辽阔，气候类型多样，资源丰富。为了进行分级管理，国家实行四级行政区域划分。在这一章里，我们来了解一下中国的地理、中国的气候、中国的资源和中国的行政区划。

第一节 中国的地理

一、中国的位置与面积

中国位于东经73度40分到东经135度5分之间，北纬4度和北纬53度31分之间，所以说，中国位于东半球、北半球，亚洲大陆的东部，太平洋的西岸。中国的陆地面积约960万平方公里，仅次于俄罗斯和加拿大，排在世界第三位，居于亚洲第一位，接近于整个欧洲的面积。

中国的领土，北起漠河以北的黑龙江主航道中心线，南到南沙群岛的曾母暗沙，南北相距约5,500公里；东起黑龙江与乌苏里江的汇合处，西到新疆维吾尔自治区的帕米尔高原，东西相距约5,200公里。

Chapter 1　China's Territory

China covers a vast territory, and there are many different types of climate. It is abundant in resources. The state government, for the purpose of hierarchical management, divides administrative areas into four levels. In this chapter, let's learn Chinese geography, Chinese climate, Chinese resources and Chinese administrative divisions.

Section 1　China's Geography

一、China's Location and Area

China is located between 73 degrees 40 and 135 degrees 5 east longitude and between 4 degrees and 53 degrees 31 north latitude, so we can say, China is located in the eastern hemisphere and the northern hemisphere, in the east of the Asian continent, on the west bank of the Pacific Ocean. The land area of China is about 9.6 million square kilometers, only less than Russia and Canada, ranking the third in the world, the first in Asia, close to the size of the whole Europe.

The Chinese territory, in the north, begins from the main channel of Heilongjiang River to the north of Mohe; in the south , to the Zengmu Reef of the Spratly Islands, and it is about 5,500 kilometers from the south to the north. In the east it starts from the confluence of the Heilongjiang River and the Wusuli River; in

中国的陆地边界长度为 22,800 公里，周围与 14 个国家相接。它们是：朝鲜、俄罗斯、蒙古、哈萨克斯坦、吉尔吉斯斯坦、塔吉克斯坦、阿富汗、巴基斯坦、印度、尼泊尔、不丹、缅甸、老挝、越南。邻近的国家还有韩国、日本、菲律宾、马来西亚、新加坡、印度尼西亚、泰国、柬埔寨、孟加拉国等。

二、中国的海洋与岛屿

中国有四大领海：从北向南依次是：渤海、黄海、东海、南海。

中国的大陆海岸线总长约 18,000 公里，岛屿海岸线总长约 14,000 公里。

中国著名的港口城市从北向南有：大连、天津、烟台、青岛、上海、厦门、深圳、广州。

中国的大小岛屿共有 6,500 多个，总面积 8 万多平方公里。其中，最大的岛屿是台湾岛，面积 35,883 平方公里。第二大岛为海南岛，面积 33,000 多平方公里。

台湾岛是中国最大的岛屿。

台湾岛的地理位置：台湾位于中国大陆东南沿海的大陆架上，东临太平洋，西隔台湾海峡与福建省相望。台湾岛面积 35,882.6258 平方公里，是中国第一大岛。

台湾的历史：其主要少数民族是高山族，在 17 世纪汉族移入前即已在此定居；明朝末年，中国台湾被荷兰和西班牙侵占；1662 年郑成功收复台湾；1895 年清政府在甲午战争中战败，与日本签订《马关条约》，把中国台湾割让给了日本；1945 年抗战胜利后光复；1949 年国民党政府在内战失利后退守台湾，海峡两岸分治至今。

the west, to the Pamirs Plateau of the Xinjiang Uygur Autonomous Region, and it extends about 5,200 kilometers from the east to the west.

China's land boundary length is about 22,800 kilometers, and it borders on 14 countries. They are: Korea, Russia, Mongolia, Kazakhstan, Kyrgyzstan, Tadzhikistan, Afghanistan, Pakistan, India, Nepal, Bhutan, Myanmar, Laos, Vietnam. Its adjacent countries have still the South Korea, Japan, Philippines, Malaysia, Singapore, Indonesia, Thailand, Cambodia, Bangladesh and so on.

二、China's Oceans and Islands

China has four major territorial waters : from north to south: the Bohai Sea, the Yellow Sea, the East China Sea, and the South China Sea.

The total length of the China's mainland coastline is about 18,000 kilometers, and the total length of the China's island coastline is about 14,000 kilometers.

The famous port cities in China from north to south: Dalian, Tianjin, Yantai, Qingdao, Shanghai, Xiamen, Shenzhen, Guangzhou.

There are altogether more than 6,500 big and small islands in China, and its total acreage is more than 80,000 square kilometers. Among them, the biggest island is the Taiwan Island, and its proportion is 35,883 square kilometers. The second biggest island is the Hainan Island, and its acreage is more than 33,000 square kilometers.

Taiwan Island is the biggest island in China.

Taiwan's geographic position: Taiwan is located on the continental shelf off the southeast coast of Chinese mainland, facing the Pacific on the east, and on the west it is separated by Taiwan Strait from Fujian Province. The acreage of Taiwan Island is 35,882.6258 square kilometers, and it is the largest island in China.

Taiwan's history: Taiwan's main ethnic minority is the Gaoshan Tribe, and they had inhabited the island before Han ethnic group moved here in the seventeenth century. It was seized by Netherlands and Spain at the end of the Ming Dynasty. In the year of 1662, the national hero Zheng Chenggong recovered Taiwan. In the year of 1895, the Qing Government was defeated in the Sino-Japanese War of 1894—

台湾和大陆的关系：1949 年，国民党内战失利，蒋中正（蒋介石）率部分国民党军政人员退踞台湾，此后台湾再次陷入与中国大陆的分离状态之中。

台湾的风景区：阿里山、日月潭、澎湖湾、阳明山国家公园、中正纪念堂、台北故宫博物院。

台湾的文化名人：余光中，琼瑶，三毛，张晓风，席慕蓉。

余光中：台湾著名诗人。1928 年 10 月 21 日出生于南京。1947 年，19 岁，考入金陵大学外语系，后转入厦门大学。1948 年，20 岁，发表第一部诗集。1949 年，21 岁，迁居香港。1950 年，22 岁，5 月到达台湾，9 月考入台湾大学外文系三年级，1952 年毕业。此后，余光中在中国台湾、美国、中国香港三地的大学执教，同时进行文学创作近 70 年，是著名的诗人和散文家。2017 年 12 月 14 日，诗人在高雄医院离世，享年 90 岁。他曾自言："大陆是母亲，台湾是妻子，香港是情人，欧洲是外遇。"其诗歌代表作品就是《乡愁》。

1895, and signed the *Treaty of Shimonoseki* with Japan, and ceded China Taiwan to Japan. In the year of 1945, it was restored after the victory of the Anti-Japanese War. In the year of 1949, the Nationalist Party government retreated to Taiwan after the defeat of the civil war, and since then the two sides of the Taiwan Strait have been divided.

Relations between Taiwan and Mainland: In the year 1949, the Nationalist Party lost the civil war, and Chiang-Kai-shek led some Nationalist Party military and political personnel to retire to Taiwan. Since then Taiwan has once again fallen into a state of separation from the Chinese mainland.

Scenic spots in Taiwan: Ali Mountain, Sun-Moon Lake, Penghu Bay, Yang Ming Shan National Park, Chiang-Kai-shek Memorial Hall, National Palace Museum in Taipei.

Cultural celebrities in Taiwan: Yu Guangzhong, Qiong Yao, San Mao, Zhang Xiaofeng, Xi Murong.

Yu Guangzhong: A very famous poet, was born in Nanjing on October 21, 1928. In the year of 1947, he was 19 years old, and entered the Foreign Language Department of Jinling University, later transferred to Xiamen University. In the next year, 1948, he was 20 years old, and published his first volume of poetry. In the year of 1949, he was 21 years old, and emigrated to Hong Kong with his family. In the ensuing year of 1950, he was 22 years old, and arrived in Taiwan in May and was admitted to the third grade of the Foreign Language Department of Taiwan University in September. He graduated in the year 1952. Hereafter, he had taught English and Chinese at some universities in three places of China Tai Wan, China Hong Kong and America, and in the meantime he had engaged in the literary creation for nearly 70 years. He has been the famous contemporary poet and proser. On the fourteenth of December, 2017, the poet died in Kaohsiung Hospital, at the age of 90. He once said to himself, "Mainland is the mother, Taiwan is the wife, Hong kong is the lover, Europe is the affair." His representative work of poetry is exactly the poem *Homesickness (Nostalgia)*.

琼瑶：原名陈喆，1938 年 4 月 20 日出生于四川成都，1949 年随父母迁居台湾。中国当代著名女作家，她创作的小说和影视剧风靡海峡两岸。

三毛：原名陈懋平，后改名陈平。1943 年出生于重庆，1948 年随父母迁居台湾。中国当代著名作家，主要写作自传性的散文。1991 年 1 月 4 日，在台北荣民总医院自缢身亡，年仅 48 岁。

张晓风：1941 年出生于浙江金华，1949 年随家人一起迁居台湾。中国当代著名作家，其散文最为著名，文风非常优美。36 岁时，被台湾文学批评界推为"当代十大散文家"之一。

席慕蓉：1943 年 10 月 15 日出生于四川重庆，1949 年随家人迁居香港，1954 年又迁居台湾（慕：admire; 荣：honour; glory; flourish）。中国当代著名的画家、诗人和散文家。其诗歌非常优美，代表诗作是《一棵开花的树》。

三、中国的地形与山脉

中国大陆地形的突出特点是：西高东低，复杂多样。

中国的地形，如果从高空俯瞰，呈现出"阶梯"状。从西向东可以分为四个阶梯。

第一个阶梯是西南部的青藏高原，平均海拔 4,000 米以上，被称为"世界屋脊"。其中，喜马拉雅山上的珠穆朗玛峰，海拔 8,844 米，是世界最高峰。

Qiong Yao: Her autonym is Chen Zhe. She was born on April 20,1938, in Chengdu, Sichuan Province, and moved to Taiwan with her parents in the year of 1949. She is a very famous contemporary Chinese writer, and her novels, movies and television plays have swept around the both sides of the Taiwan Strait.

San Mao: Her autonym is Chen Maoping. Later, she changed her name to Chen Ping. She was born in Chongqing in the year of 1943, and moved to Taiwan with her parents in the year of 1948. She was also a very famous contemporary Chinese writer, and she mainly wrote the autobiographical proses. She hung herself in Taipei's Rongmin General Hospital on January 4, 1991, only 48 years old.

Zhang Xiaofeng: She was born in the year of 1941 in the city Jinhua, Zhejiang Province, and moved to Taiwan with her parents in the year of 1949. She is also a very famous contemporary Chinese writer, and her proses are the most prominent. The style of her proses is very beautiful. She was chosen as one of the top ten contemporary prosers by the Taiwan literary critics when she was 36 years old.

Xi Murong: She was born on October 15, 1943, in Chongqing, Sichuan Province, and moved to Hong Kong with her parents in the year of 1949, then moved to Taiwan in the year of 1954. She is also a very famous contemporary painter, poet and proser. Her poems are very beautiful, and her representative poem is *One Flowering Tree*.

三、China's Topography and Mountains

The outstanding characteristics of the China's mainland topography are as follows: higher in the west and lower in the east , complex and varied.

The Chinese topography, if overlooked from a great height, presents the ladder form. From the west to the east, it can be divided into the four ladders .

The first ladder is the Qinghai-Tibet Plateau in the southwest, whose average elevation is more than 4,000 meters, and also called the roof of the world. Among them, the summit of the Mount Everest in the Himalayas, whose elevation is 8,844 meters, is the highest summit in the world.

第二阶梯是向东的高原、盆地和沙漠，海拔为 2000~1000 米。

第三阶梯向东直达海岸，主要是丘陵和平原，平均海拔下降到 1000~500 米。自北向南的三大平原是：东北平原，华北平原，长江中下游平原。

第四阶梯是中国大陆伸向海洋的大陆架，海水较浅，大部分不到 200 米。

四、中国的河流与湖泊

因为中国大陆地形的特点是西高东低，所以，中国的大江大河基本都是从西向东流。

世界四大河流：

尼罗河，长 6,671 公里，位于非洲。流经：卢旺达、布隆迪、坦桑尼亚、肯尼亚、乌干达、扎伊尔、苏丹、埃塞俄比亚和埃及 9 个国家，最终注入地中海，是世界上流经国家最多的国际性河流之一。

亚马孙河，长 6,480 公里，南美洲。

长江，长 6,300 公里，亚洲，中国及亚洲第一大河。

密西西比河，长 6,260 公里，北美洲。

中国最长的四大河流：

长江，全长 6,300 公里，发源于青藏高原，流入东海，中国第一大河。

中国的第二大河：黄河，全长 5,464 公里，发源于青海省的巴颜喀拉山，流入渤海。

中国的第三大河：黑龙江，全长 4,440 公里，是中国与俄罗斯的界河。

The second stair is the eastern plateaus, basins and deserts, and its altitude is from 2,000 meters to 1,000 meters.

The third step is eastern to the coast, and it is mainly the uplands and plains, and its elevation descends between 1,000 meters and 500 meters. From north to south, the three biggest plains are the Northeast Plain, the North China Plain, and the Middle-lower Yangtze Plain.

The fourth stile is the continental shelf that extends to the ocean from the Chinese mainland, and its seawater is more shallow, most of which is less than two hundred meters.

四、China's Rivers and Lakes

Because the topographic characteristic of Chinese mainland is higher in the west and lower in the east, the Chinese big rivers basically flow from west to east.

The four longest rivers in the world are as follows.

The Nile River: 6,671 kilometers long, in Africa, flowing through 9 countries (Rwanda, Burundi, Tanzania, Kenya, Uganda, Zaire, Sudan, Ethiopia and Egypt) into the Mediterranean, one of the international rivers that flow through the most countries in the world.

The Amazon River: 6,480 kilometers long, in the South America.

The Yangtze River: 6,300 kilometers long, in China, Asia, the longest river in Asia.

The Mississippi River: 6,260 kilometers long, in the North America.

The four longest rivers in China are as follows.

The longest river in China is the Yangtze River, and whose overall length is 6,300 kilometers, originating from the Qinghai-Tibet Plateau, flowing into the East China Sea.

The second longest river in China is the Yellow River, and whose overall length is 5,464 kilometers. It originates from the Bayan Har Mountains in Qinghai Province, and flows into the Bohai Sea.

The third longest river in China is the Heilongjiang River, whose overall length

中国的第四大河：珠江，全长 2,197 公里，流入南海。

中国的四大淡水湖：江西的鄱（pó）阳湖、湖南的洞庭湖、江苏的太湖和洪泽湖。

中国最大的内陆湖：青海湖，面积 4,583 平方公里，咸水湖。

第二节　中国的气候

中国的气候特征：四季分明，雨热同季；冬季寒冷干燥，夏季大部分地区降雨较多。

中国气候类型复杂多样，主要有以下五种。

一、热带季风气候

包括台湾省的南部、雷州半岛和海南岛等地。年积温≥8000℃，最冷月份平均气温不低于 16℃，年极端最低气温多年平均不低于 5℃，极端最低气温一般不低于 0℃，终年无霜。

is 4,440 kilometers, and is the boundary river between China and Russia.

The fourth longest river is the Pearl River, whose overall length is 2,197 kilometers, and flows into the South China Sea.

The four major freshwater lakes in China are the Poyang Lake in Jiangxi Province, the Dongting Lake in Hunan Province, the Taihu Lake and the Hongze Lake in Jiangsu Province.

The largest inland lake in China is Qinghai Lake, and whose acreage is 4,583 square kilometers, a salt water lake.

Section 2 China's Climate

The climate characteristics of China are: The four seasons are distinct, and the rainy season coincides with the high temperature; it is cold and dry in winter, and it rains more in most parts of China in summer.

China's climate types are complex and diverse, and there are five main types.

一、Tropical Monsoon Climate

The Tropical Monsoon Climate includes the southern part of Taiwan Province, Leizhou Peninsula, Hainan Island and other places. The annual cumulative temperature is greater than or equal to $8,000\,°C$, and the average temperature in the coldest months is not less than $16\,°C$. The annual extremely minimum temperature has not been less than $5\,°C$ on average for many years. The extremely minimun temperature is generally not less than $0\,°C$, frost-free throughout the year.

二、亚热带季风气候

我国华北和华南地区属于此种类型的气候。年积温在 4500~8000℃，最冷月平均气温是 –8~0℃，是副热带与温带之间的过渡地带，夏季气温相当高，冬季气温相当低。

三、温带季风气候

我国内蒙古和新疆北部等地属于此种类型的气候。年积温在 1600~3400℃，最冷月平均气温在 –28~8℃。夏季平均气温多数仍超过 22℃，但超过 25℃的已很少见。

四、温带大陆性气候

广义的温带大陆性气候包括温带沙漠气候、温带草原气候及亚寒带针叶林气候。狭义的温带大陆性气候只包括温带沙漠气候和温带草原气候，不包括湿润的亚寒带针叶林气候。我国北纬 30° 以北的大部分内陆地区都是温带大陆性气候。

五、高原山地气候

我国青藏高原及一些高山地区属于此种气候类型。年积温低于 2000℃，日平均气温低于 10℃。日气温温差较大而年气温温差较小，但太阳辐射强，日照充足。

二、Subtropical Monsoon Climate

The North and South China belongs to the Subtropical Monsoon Climate. The annual cumulative temperature is between 4,500℃ and 8,000℃, while the average temperature in the coldest months is between -8℃ and 0℃. It is the transition zone between the subtropic zone and the temperate zone. The temperature is quite high in summer, and quite low in winter.

三、Temperate Monsoon Climate

China's Inner Mongolia and northern Xinjiang and other places belong to the type of climate. The annual cumulative temperature is between 1,600℃ and 3,400℃. The average temperature in the coldest months is between -28℃ and 8℃. The average summer temperature remains above 22℃ for the most part, but it has been rare that the average summer temperature is above twenty-five degrees Celcius.

四、Temperate Continental Climate

The broad sense of the Temperate Continental Climate includes the Temperate Desert Climate, the Temperate Grassland Climate and the Subfrigid Coniferous Forest Climate. In the narrow sense, the Temperate Continental Climate only includes the Temperate Desert Climate and the Temperate Grassland Climate, excluding the humid Subfrigid Coniferous Forest Climate. Most of the inland areas north of 30° north latitude is the Temperate Continental Climate.

五、Plateau and Mountain Climate

The Qinghai-Tibet Plateau and some alpine areas belong to this type of climate. The annual cumulative temperature is less than 2,000℃. The average daily temperature is below 10℃. The daily temperature difference is larger and the annual

第三节　中国的资源

一、中国的土地资源

中国的土地类型有三大特点：一是山地多，平地少；二是干旱、半干旱地区占的比重较大；三是土地资源分布不平衡。

中国最著名的天然牧场是内蒙古大草原，面积近 87 万平方公里，占全国天然草场的四分之一。

二、中国的生物资源

中国特有的珍贵动物有一百多种：大熊猫、金丝猴、台湾猴、牛羚、梅花鹿、白唇鹿、白鳍豚、扬子鳄、中华鲟、白鲟等。

中国的珍稀鸟类有：朱鹮、丹顶鹤、白鹤、黑鹳、天鹅、黄腹角雉、白冠长尾雉等。

中国特有的树木：银杏、水杉、水松、银杉、金钱松、台湾松、福建柏、珙桐、杜仲等。

temperature difference is smaller. But the sun radiates strongly and it can get plenty of sunshine.

Section 3 China's Resources

一、China's Land Resources

The China's land types have three major characteristics: the first one is that the mountainous region is more, and the flat ground is less; the second one is that the arid and the semi-arid areas account for a larger proportion; the third one is that the distribution of the land resources is unbalanced.

The most famous natural pasture in China is the Inner Mongolia Prairie, and its acreage is nearly 870,000 square kilometers, accounting for a quarter of the national natural pasture.

二、China's Biological Resources

The China's unique and precious animals are more than one hundred kinds, including the Giant Panda, the Golden Monkey, the Macaca Cyclopis, the Gnu, the Sika Deer, the White-lipped Deer, the White-flag Dolphin, the Yangtze Alligator, the Chinese Sturgeon, the Paddlefish, etc.

The China's rare birds include the Crested Ibis, the Red-crowned Crane, the White Crane, the Black Stork, the Swan, the Yellow-bellied Tragopan Caboti, the Reeves's Pheasant, etc.

The China's unique trees include Gingko, Metasequoia, the Chinese Cypress (the Huon Pine), the Silver Fir, the Golden Larch, the Pinus Taiwanensis Hayata,

三、中国的矿产资源

1. 能源矿产

中国的主要能源是煤炭，预测蕴藏量达到 45,000 亿吨，储量和产量都占世界第一位。中国的第二大能源是石油。

2. 黑色金属矿产

中国的黑色金属矿产主要是铁矿。中国铁矿的分布比较普遍，已探明储量 450 亿吨，居世界第三位。

3. 有色金属矿产

有色金属，是指所有的非铁合金金属。中国的有色金属矿产主要是金矿、铜矿、铅矿、锌矿和钨矿。金矿储量居世界第四位，铜矿储量居世界第三位，铅矿、锌矿和钨矿均居世界第一位。

第四节 中国的行政区划

中国现行的行政区划是，全国划分为省、市（地）、县、乡镇四级。其中，省一级的行政区包括省、自治区、直辖市、特别行政区四种。目前，全国共有 34 个省级行政区，包括：23 个省、4 个直辖市、5 个自治区、2 个特别行政区。

the Fokienia Hodginsii, the Davidia Involucrate, the Eucommia Ulmoides and so on.

三、China's Mineral Resources

1. Energy Minerals

China's major energy is coal. It is forecasted that its reserves reach 4.5 trillion tons, and both its reserves and production rank the first in the world. The second major energy in China is petroleum.

2. Black Metal Mineral

China's black metal mineral is mainly the iron ore, and the distribution of china's iron ore is more widespread. Its reserves that have been ascertained are 45 billion tons, and rank the third in the world.

3. Nonferrous Metal Minerals

The nonferrous metals mean all the nonferrous alloying metals. China's nonferrous metal minerals are mainly the gold ore, the copper ore, the lead ore, the zinc ore and the tungsten ore. China's gold reserves rank the fourth in the world, and the copper reserves rank the third in the world. The reserves of the lead ore, the zinc ore and the tungsten ore all rank the first in the world.

Section 4 China's Administrative Division

China's current administrative divisions (regionalization) are as follows: the whole country is divided into four levels—province, municipality (district), county and township. Among them, the provincial administrative regions include the four kinds: provinces, autonomous regions, municipalities directly under the central

23 个省：黑龙江省、吉林省、辽宁省、山东省、江苏省、浙江省、福建省、广东省、海南省、云南省、甘肃省、河北省、河南省、安徽省、江西省、湖南省、湖北省、山西省、陕西省、贵州省、四川省、青海省、台湾省。

4 个直辖市：北京市、上海市、天津市、重庆市。

5 个自治区：西藏自治区、新疆维吾尔自治区、内蒙古自治区、宁夏回族自治区、广西壮族自治区。

2 个特别行政区：香港特别行政区、澳门特别行政区。

关于香港：香港一直是中国的领土。1840 年之前的香港还是一个小渔村。1842—1997 年，香港沦为英国殖民地。1997 年 7 月 1 日，中国政府正式恢复对香港行使主权，建立香港特别行政区。中国政府允许香港保留原有的经济模式、法律和社会制度，并可享有外交及国防以外所有事务的高度自治权。

关于澳门：澳门一直是中国的领土。1553 年，葡萄牙人取得澳门居住权。1887 年 12 月 1 日，葡萄牙政府与清朝政府签订《中葡会议草约》和《中葡和好通商条约》，正式通过外交文书的手续占领了澳门并将其辟为殖民

government, and special administrative regions. At present, China has altogether 34 provincial-level administrative regions including 23 provinces throughout the country, 4 direct-controlled municipalities, 5 autonomous regions, and 2 special administrative regions.

The 23 provinces are: Heilongjiang Province, Jilin Province, Liaoning Province, Shandong Province, Jiangsu Province, Zhejiang Province, Fujian Province, Guangdong Province, Hainan Province, Yunnan Province, Gansu Province, Hebei Province, Henan Province, Anhui Province, Jiangxi Province, Hunan Province, Hubei Province, Shanxi Province, Shaanxi Province, Guizhou Province, Sichuan Province, Qinghai Province, and Taiwan Province.

The 4 direct-controlled municipalities are: Beijing, Shanghai, Tianjin, and Chongqing.

The 5 autonomous regions are: the Tibet Autonomous Region, the Xinjiang Uygur Autonomous Region, the Inner Mongolia Autonomous Region, the Ningxia Hui Autonomous Region and the Guangxi Zhuang Autonomous Region.

The 2 special administrative regions are: Hong Kong Special Administrative Region and Macao Special Administrative Region.

About Hong Kong: Hong Kong has always been the Chinese territory. Hong Kong had been a small fishing village before 1840. Hong Kong had become into a British colony from 1842 to 1997. On the first of July, 1997, the Chinese government officially resumed the exercise of sovereignty over Hong Kong, and established the Hong Kong Special Administrative Region. The Chinese government has allowed Hong Kong to retain its own original economic model, legal and social systems, and enjoy a high degree of autonomy in all matters other than foreign affairs and national defence.

About Macao: Macao has also been the Chinese Territory in all ages. In the year 1553, the Portuguese obtained the right of habitation in Macao. On the first of December, 1887, the Portuguese government and the Qing government signed

地。1999 年 12 月 20 日，中国政府恢复对澳门行使主权，建立澳门特别行政区，像香港一样，实行"一国两制"的政策。

我国有这么多的省、市、自治区，但是，90% 的中国人都不知道它们名称的由来。

北京

战国时期称蓟，是"战国七雄"之一燕国的京城。辽国称燕京。金国改称京都。元朝称大都。明朝朱元璋改称北平，永乐帝朱棣改北平为北京。简称京。

天津

明朝时，燕王为争夺皇位，在这里发兵渡河南下，打败他的侄子明惠帝而篡了位。为纪念在这里渡河起兵，所以称之为"天津"，意即天子经过的渡口，简称津。

上海

北宋初期，这里已形成居民点，从这里上海洋，所以称上海。上海原来是捕鱼的地方，当时渔民创造了一种捕鱼工具，叫"扈"（扈由竹子编成，插在水中捕鱼）。后来"扈"改为"沪"，所以上海简称"沪"。

重庆

隋文帝开皇元年（582 年），以渝水（嘉陵江古称）绕城，改楚州为渝

the *Sino-Portuguese Conference Protocol* and the *Sino-Portuguese Treaty of Amity and Commerce*, and Portugal formally occupied Macao through the procedures of diplomatic documents, and made it a colony. On the 20th Dec, 1999, the Chinese government resumed the exercise of sovereignty over Macao, and established the Macao Special Administratvie Region. Like in Hong Kong, the policy in Macao is "One Country, Two Systems". ("One Country" means the People's Republic of China, and "Two Systems" mean the socialist system and the capitalist system.)

There are so many provinces, municipalities and autonomous regions in China, but about 90% of the Chinese people don't know the derivations of the names of our country's provinces and municipalities.

Beijing was named Ji (thistle) during the Warring States Period, and it was the capital of Yan State, one of the seven powers in the Warring States Period. It was called Yan Jing by Liao State. It was renamed Jing Du by Jin State. It was termed Da Du by Yuan Dynasty. It was intituled Bei Ping by the Emperor of Ming Dynasty, Zhu Yuanzhang. Later, the Emperor Zhu Di, Whose reign title was Yong Le, changed Bei Ping to Beijing. It is called Jing for short.

Tianjin: In the Ming Dynasty, in order to fight for the throne, the King of Yan dispatched troops from here to cross the river to march south, and defeated his nephew the Emperor Minghui and succeeded him. In memory of raising an army and crossing the river at this place, it was called Tian Jin, namely, it was the the ferry through which the Emperor passed. It is called Jin for short.

Shanghai: In the early Nothern Song Dynasty, the residential areas had been formed here. People went to the sea from here, so it was called Shanghai. Shanghai was originally a place for fishing, and at that time, the fishermen created a kind of fishing tool, called Yong. It was woven from bamboo and inserted in water. Later, Yong was changed to Hu, and Shanghai was shortened to Hu.

Chongqing: In the first year of the Emperor Wen of Sui Dynasty, whose reign title was Kai Huang, because the Yu River (the ancient name of Jia Ling River)

州。这就是重庆简称"渝"的来历。北宋孝宗淳熙十六年（1189 年），皇子赵接踵于正月封恭王，二月受内禅即帝位，自诩"双重喜庆"，遂将恭州（重庆原名）升格命名为重庆府。重庆得名迄今已八百余年。

黑龙江省

由黑龙江而得名。因为江水呈黑绿色，蜿蜒地流着像条游龙，故称黑龙江，简称黑。

吉林省

清政府在松花江沿岸建立吉林乌拉城（今吉林市）。满语"吉林"是"沿"的意思，乌拉是"大川"的意思，吉林乌拉城就是沿着松花江的城市。后来建省时，就用吉林省来命名，简称吉。

辽宁省

由于它在辽河流域，取辽河永久安宁之意，简称辽。

河北省

相对于黄河为北。唐朝时，黄河以北、太行山以东的地区为河北道。1928 年称河北省。因古代属冀州地区，所以简称冀。

河南省

相对于黄河为南，主要部分在黄河以南。因为古代属豫州地区，所以简称豫。

陕西省

是指现在的河南省陕县西南陕陌以西的地区，简称陕。古代时是秦国领土，又简称秦。

encircled (surrounded) the city, the city Chu Zhou was changed to Yu Zhou, and this was the derivation that the city Chongqing was shortened as Yu. In the sixteenth year of the Emperor Xiao Zong whose reign title was Chun Xi, the prince Zhao Jiezhong was conferred the King of Gong in the first month of the lunar year, and accepted the crown handed over by the former emperor within the family in the lunar February. He boasted of the double happiness, and then upgraded Gong Zhou (formerly known as Chongqing) as the Prefecutre of Chongqing. Chongqing has gotten its name for more than eight hundred years.

Heilongjiang Province has gotten its name from the Heilongjiang River, because the water in the river presents the dark green color, and it meanders like a swimming dragon. It is called Hei for short.

Jilin Province: The Qing Dynasty established the Jilin Ullah City (present-day Jilin City) along the Song Hua River. In Manchu language, the word Jilin means along, and Ullah means large river. Jilin Ullah City means the city along the Song Hua River. Later, when the province was established, Jilin Province was used for the name, while Ji is called for short.

Liaoning Province: Because it is in the Liaohe River Basin, and the meaning of Liaohe River's permanent peace is adopted. It is called Liao for short.

Hebei Province is in the north of Yellow River. During the Tang Dynasty, the area between the north of Yellow River and the east of Taihang Mountain was Hebei Dao. In the year 1928, it was called as Hebei Province. Because it belonged to the Jizhou Region in ancient times, it has been called Ji for short.

Henan Province: Because it is on the south of Yellow River, namely, its main part is south of the Yellow River, it is called as Henan Province. Because it belonged to the Yu Zhou Region in ancient times, it has been called Yu for short.

Shaanxi Province refers to the area west of Shan Mo, southwest of Shan County, Henan Province. It is called Shan for short. It belonged to the territory of Qin State in ancient times, and it is also called Qin for short.

甘肃省

是以古代甘州（今张掖）和肃州（今酒泉）的头一个字组成，简称甘。境内的六盘山又叫陇山，故又简称陇。

山西省

相对于太行山为西。明朝设置山西省，春秋时是晋国领土，所以简称晋。

山东省

相对于太行山为东。明朝设置山东省，春秋时是鲁国领土，所以简称鲁。

湖南省

相对于洞庭湖为南。由于湘江纵贯全省，所以简称湘。

湖北省

相对于洞庭湖为北。清朝时省会武昌属鄂州管辖，所以简称鄂。

江苏省

是以清朝时的江宁府（今南京市）和苏州府（今苏州市）的头一个字组成。简称苏。

浙江省

境内的浙江盘桓曲折，所以称为浙江省。浙江就是富春江。简称浙。

安徽省

以清朝时的安庆府（今安庆）和徽州府（今歙县）的头一字组成。因境内有皖山（天柱山），因而简称皖。

江西省

唐朝为江南西道，简称江西道。清朝时改为江西省。因赣江纵贯全省，所以简称赣。

Gansu Province's name is made up of the first character of the two cities Gan zhou (present-day Zhangye) and Suzhou (present-day Jiuquan). It is called Gan for short, within which there is a Liupan Mountain, also called Long Mountain, so it is also called Long for short.

Shanxi Province is west of Taihang Mountain, which was set up in Ming Dynasty. Because it belonged to the territory of Jin State during the Spring and Autumn Period, it has been called Jin for short.

Shandong Province is east of Taihang Mountain, which was set up in Ming Dynasty. Because it belonged to the territory of Lu State during the Spring and Autumn Period, it has been called Lu for short.

Hunan Province is south of Dongting Lake. Because the Xiangjiang River stretches across the whole province, it has been called Xiang for short.

Hubei Province is north of Dongting Lake. Because in the Qing Dynasty, the provincial capital Wuchang was administered by E State, it has been called E for short.

Jiangsu Province's name is made up of the first character of the two prefectures—Jiangning (present-day Nanjing City), and Suzhou (present-day Suzhou City) in the Qing Dynasty. It has been called Su for short.

Zhejiang Province: Within the province, a river called Zhe, twists and turns. The Zhe River is exact the Fuchun River. It has been called Zhe for short.

Anhui Province's name is made up of the first character of the two prefectures of the Qing Dynasty—Anqing (present-day Anqing City) and Huizhou (present-day Xi County). Because there is a mountain named Wan Mountain, it has been called Wan for short.

Jiangxi Province: In the Tang Dynasty, it was called Jiang Nan Xi Dao, and Jiang Xi Dao for short. In the Qing Dynasty, it was changed to Jiang Xi Province. Because the Gan River flows throughout the entire province, it has been called Gan for short.

福建省

古代设福州、建州、泉州、漳州、汀州五个州，取前两个州的头一个字就是福建。明朝设福建省，因是闽族人居住地区，所以简称闽。

广东省

五代时叫广东。明朝设广东省。因为这里古代是百越（粤）地区，所以简称粤。

贵州省

明朝设置贵州省。简称贵。因为这里古代属黔中郡，所以简称黔。

四川省

唐朝初年，现在的四川省剑阁以南设东川，西川。这里的川，是平川广野的意思。宋代分设利州、益州、梓州和夔州四路，合称"川峡四路"，简称四川。元朝设四川省，简称川。三国时是蜀国领土，所以也简称蜀。

云南省

因在云岭以南而得名。相传汉武帝时有人在白崖看见彩云，并派人追彩云到这里。因为设立的县在彩云的边上，所以叫云南，简称云。因为昆明附近是古代滇国，故又简称滇。

青海省

因青海湖而得名。1928 年建青海省，简称青。

Fujian Province: In ancient times the five states were set up including Fuzhou, Jianzhou, Quanzhou, Zhangzhou and Tingzhou; the province's name adopted the initials of the first two states, namely, Fuzhou and Jianzhou. In Ming Dynasty Fujian Province was set up. Because this area has been the region where the people of Min ethnic group have lived, it has been called Min for short.

Guangdong Province: It was called Guang Dong during the Five Dynasties period. In Ming Dynasty Guangdong Province was set up. Because this area was the Bai Yue region in ancient times, it has been called Yue for short.

Guizhou Province: In Ming Dynasty Guizhou Province was set up. It has been called Gui for short. Because it belonged to the prefecture of Qianzhong in ancient times, it has also been called Qian for short.

Sichuan Province: The early Tang Dynasty set up Dong Chuan and Xi Chuan in the south of Jian'ge of present-day Sichuan. Here, Chuan means the boundless plain. Later, the Song Dynasty set up the Si Lu including Li Zhou, Yi Zhou, Zi Zhou and Kui Zhou, therefore this area was called Chuan Xia Si Lu. It was called Sichuan for short. In Yuan Dynasty Sichuan Province was set up, and was called Chuan for short. It belonged to the territory of the Shu State during the Three Kingdoms period, also called Shu for short.

Yunnan Province has gotten its name because it is in the south of Yun Ling. According to the local legend, during the Emperor Wudi of the Han Dynasty, some people saw the colorful clouds on the White Cliff, and the Emperor sent some people to chase the colorful clouds here. Because the county was set up on the edge of the colorful clouds, it was called Yunnan. It has been called Yun for short. Because the area nearby the provincial capital Kunming belonged to the Dian State in ancient times, it has also been called Dian for short.

Qinghai Province has gotten its name because of the Qinghai Lake. The Qinghai Province was set up in the year of 1928. It has been called Qing for short.

讨论题：

你们已经来中国一段时间了，请谈谈你对中国的印象。可以从中国的地理、中国的历史、中国的民众、中国的民族、中国的习俗、中国的艺术、中国的旅游景点、中国的国际形象、中国人的精神气质以及中国的发展前景等话题中任选一个谈谈。

Discussion Question:

You have been in China for a period of time. Please talk about your impression about China. You can choose any one of the following topics: Chinese geography, Chinese history, Chinese people, Chinese ethnic groups, Chinese customs, Chinese arts, Chinese tourist attractions, the international image of China, the spirit and temperament of the Chinese people and the prospect of China's development, etc.

第二章　中国的历史

　　中国是世界上四大文明古国（中国、古印度、古埃及、古巴比伦）之一，已有大约五千多年的历史。中国历史经过了原始社会（约公元前170万年—前21世纪）、奴隶社会（约公元前2070年—前476年）、封建社会（公元前475年—1840年）、半殖民地半封建社会（1840—1949年）。1949年以后，中国开始进入社会主义社会。

第一节　中国古代史（1840年以前）

一、原始社会时期（公元前170万年—前21世纪）

　　根据考古资料，大约一百万年以前，中国已经有了原始人类。在云南省元谋县发现了元谋人化石，在陕西省蓝田县发现了蓝田人化石，他们是已知的中国最早的原始人类。大约四五十万年以前，在北京周口店一带生活的"北京猿人"，具备了人的基本特征。

Chapter 2　History of China

China is one of the four great ancient civilizations in the world. The four great ancient civilizations included China, ancient India, ancient Egypt and ancient Babylonia. China has had a history of more than five thousand years. The Chinese history has passed the Primitive Society (from about 1.7 million B.C.to the twenty-first century B.C.), the Slave Society (about 2070 B.C.—476 B.C.), the Feudal Society (475 B.C.—1840), the Semi-colonial and Semi-feudal Society (1840—1949). After 1949, China began to enter into the Socialist Society.

Section 1　Ancient History of China (Before 1840)

一、The Primitive Society (1.7 Million B.C.—the Twenty-first Century B.C.)

According to the archaeological data, about one million years ago, China had the primitive humans (the hominid). The Yuanmou Man Fossil that was found in Yuanmou County, Yunnan Province, and the Lantian Man Fossil that was found in Lantian County, Shaanxi Province, were the earliest known Chinese hominids. About four or five hundred thousand years ago, the Peking Man (the sinanthropus pekinensis, the homo erectus pekinensis) who lived in Beijing Zhoukoudian area had the basic characteristics of modern people.

中国原始人类曾经历了母系氏族公社和父系氏族公社两个发展阶段。六七千年以前，在黄河流域和长江流域出现的"仰韶文化"是母系氏族公社的代表。五千年以前，在黄河流域出现的"龙山文化"是父系氏族公社的代表。

原始社会末期，以黄帝为首的部落比较强大。因此，黄帝被说成是中华民族的始祖。因为炎帝与黄帝结盟，所以，中华民族又称为"炎黄子孙"。黄帝陵在陕西省黄陵县。炎帝陵有两处，一处在湖南省炎陵县，另一处在陕西省宝鸡市南面。

二、奴隶社会时期——夏、商、西周（公元前 2070 年—前 771 年）

中国的奴隶社会，从公元前的 2070 年到公元前的 771 年，经历了夏、商、西周三个朝代。

夏朝：公元前 21 世纪建立，是中国历史上最早的奴隶制国家，从禹开始到桀灭亡，历时 470 年。

商朝：公元前 16 世纪建立，约公元前 1046 年灭亡，历时 554 年。产生了文字。

西周：大约公元前 11 世纪建立，公元前 771 年覆亡，历时 275 年。

三、奴隶社会向封建社会的过渡时期——春秋、战国时期（大约公元前 770 年—前 221 年）

公元前 771 年，西周灭亡。次年，周平王迁都到洛邑（今天河南洛阳），

The Chinese primitive (original) human had once experienced the two stages of development including the Matriarchal Clan Commune and Patriarchal Clan Commune. About six or seven thousand years ago, the Yangshao Culture that appeared in the Yellow River basin and the Yangtze River basin was the representative of the Matriarchal Clan Commune. Five thousand years ago, the Longshan Culture that appeared in the Yellow River basin was the representative of the Patriarchal Clan Commune.

In the late Primitive Society, the tribe headed by the Huang Emperor was stronger. Therefore, the Huang Emperor was said to be the earliest ancestor of the Chinese Nation. Because the Yan Emperor allied with the Huang Emperor, the Chinese Nation has been also known as the descendants of the Yan and Huang Emperors. The mausoleum of Huang Emperor is in the Huangling County, Shaanxi Province. There are two mausoleums of Yan Emperor, one is in the Yanling County, Hunan province, and the other is south of Baoji City, Shaanxi province.

二、The Period of the Slave Society–Xia, Shang, West Zhou Dynasty (2070B.C.—771B.C.)

The Slave Society of China was from 2070 B.C. to 771 B.C., and it experienced the three dynasties including Xia, Shang and West Zhou Dynasties.

The Xia Dynasty was founded in the twenty-first century B.C., and it was the earliest slave-owner's state. The Xia Dynasty lasted 470 years, from the beginning of Yu to the death of Jie.

The Shang Dynasty was founded in the sixteenth century B.C., and ended in about 1046 B.C.. It lasted for 554 years and produced the Chinese characters.

The West Zhou Dynasty was founded in about the eleventh century B.C., and fell in 771 B.C.. It lasted for 275 years.

三、The Period of Transition from Slave Society to Feudal Society——the Spring and Autumn Period and the Warring States Period (about 770B.C.—221B.C.)

In 771 B.C., the West Zhou Dynasty died out (perished). In the second year

开始了东周时期。东周又分为"春秋时期"（公元前 770 年—前 476 年）和"战国时期"（公元前 475 年—前 221 年）两个时期。

战国七雄：齐国、楚国、燕国、韩国、赵国、魏国、秦国。

百家争鸣：以孔子为代表的儒家学派，以老子和庄子为代表的道家学派，以商鞅和韩非子为代表的法家学派，以墨子为代表的墨家学派。

四、封建国家的建立和巩固时期——从秦朝到东汉（公元前 221 年—220 年）

从秦王朝的建立，到东汉末年，大约 440 年，是中国封建社会的巩固时期。

公元前 221 年，秦始皇建立了秦朝，这是中国历史上第一个封建国家。大家知道，秦始皇修筑了长城。秦始皇和秦二世，仅仅统治了 15 年，就被陈胜和吴广领导的农民大起义推翻了。

公元前 206 年，刘邦，在长安（今陕西西安）建立了西汉王朝。

公元 25 年，在洛阳，刘秀建立了东汉王朝。

(the next year, the year ensuing), the King Ping of Zhou moved the capital to the city Luoyi (present-day Luoyang City, Henan Province), and began (started, initiated) the East Zhou Period. The East Zhou Period was divided into two periods, the Spring and Autumn Period(770B.C.—476 B.C.) and the Warring States Period (475B.C.-221B.C.)

The Seven Powers in the Warring States Period included the Qi State, the Chu State, the Yan State, the Han State, the Zhao State, the Wei State and the Qin State.

Contention of One Hundred Schools of Thoughts.

All schools of thoughts contended for attention, including the Confucian School represented by Confucius, the Taoist School represented by Lao-tzu and Zhuangzi, the Legalist School represented by Shangyang and Han Feizi, and the Mohist School represented by Mo-tse.

四、The Establishment and Consolidation Period of the Feudal State—from the Qin Dynasty to the Eastern Han Dynasty(221B.C.–220A.D.)

From the establishment of the Qin Dynasty to the end of the Eastern Han Dynasty, about 440 years, was the consolidation period of the Chinese Feudal Society.

In 221 B.C., the First Emperor of Qin established the Qin Dynasty, and this was the first feudal state in the Chinese history. All of you know, the First Emperor of Qin built the Great Wall. The First Emperor of Qin and the Second Emperor of Qin ruled only fifteen years, and then the Qin Dynasty was overthrown by the great peasants' uprising led by Chen Sheng and Wu Guang.

In 206 B.C., Liu Bang established the Western Han Dynasty in Chang'an (present-day Xi'an City, Shaanxi Province).

In 25 A.D., Liu Xiu established the Eastern Han Dynasty in Luoyang.

五、封建社会的发展和鼎盛时期——从三国到唐代（220—907 年）

三国时期（220—280 年）是上承东汉下启西晋的一段历史时期。三国鼎立：魏国、蜀国、吴国。

唐朝：从 618 到 907 年，历时 289 年，是中国封建社会发展的顶峰。唐朝最有作为的皇帝是唐太宗李世民。

六、封建社会的继续发展时期——从五代十国到元代（907—1368 年）

五代十国（907—979 年）是中国历史上的一段大分裂时期。包括五代（907—960 年）与十国（902—979 年）等众多割据政权，自唐朝灭亡开始，至宋朝建立为止。也可以定义为自唐朝灭亡开始，到宋朝统一十国剩余政权为止。

五代是指 907 年唐朝灭亡后依次更替的位于中原地区的五个政权，即后梁、后唐、后晋、后汉与后周。960 年，赵匡胤篡后周建立北宋，五代结束。

在唐末、五代及宋初，中原地区之外存在过许多割据政权，其中前蜀、后蜀、吴、南唐、吴越、闽、楚、南汉、南平（荆南）、北汉共十个割据政权，被《新五代史》及后世史学家合称为"十国"。

五、The Developmental and Prosperous Period of the Feudal Society—from the Three Kingdoms Period to the Tang Dynasty (220—907)

The Three Kingdoms Period was from 220 to 280, and it was the period of the historical transition from the Eastern Han Dynasty to the Western Jin Dynasty. The tripartite confrontation of the three kingdoms: Wei State, Shu State and Wu State.

The Tang Dynasty was from 618 to 907, lasting for 279 years, and it was the highest peak of the development of the Chinese Feudal Society. The most successful emperor in Tang Dynasty was Tang Taizong Li Shimin.

六、The Continuous Development Period of the Feudal Society—from the Five Dynasties to the Yuan Dynasty (907—1368)

The Five Dynasties and Ten States Period was from 907 to 979, and it was a period of great division in Chinese history, including many locality separatist powers such as the Five Dynasties (907—960) and the Ten States(902—979). This period began from the fall of the Tang Dynasty to the establishment of the Song Dynasty. It can also be defined as the period from the collapse of the Tang Dynasty to the unification of the remaining Ten States by the Song Dynasty.

The Five Dynasties refer to the five regimes in the central plains which were successively replaced after the fall of the Tang Dynasty, namely the Later Liang Dynasty (907—923), the Later Tang Dynasty (923—936), the Later Jin Dynasty (936—946), the Later Han Dynasty (947—950), and the Later Zhou Dynasty (951—960). In 960, Zhao Kuangyin usurped the Later Zhou Dynasty and established the Northern Song Dynasty, ending the Five Dynasties.

In the periods of the Tang Dynasty, the Five Dynasties and the early Song Dynasty, there were many separatist regimes outside the central plains. Among them, the ten separatist regimes including the Former Shu, the Later Shu, the Wu, the Southern Tang, the Wu Yue, the Min, the Chu, the Southern Han, the Southern Ping

宋朝（960—1279 年）是中国历史中上承五代十国下启元朝的朝代，分北宋和南宋两个阶段，共历 18 帝，享国 319 年。

1279 年，蒙古族人成吉思汗的孙子忽必烈建立了元朝，这是中国历史上第一个由少数民族统治的王朝。

意大利威尼斯商人马可·波罗来到中国，写了一本书《马可·波罗游记》，生动地描写了当时中国社会的状况。

七、封建社会的衰落时期——明清时期（1368—1840 年）

1368 年，朱元璋建立明朝。

1644 年，满族建立清朝，这是中国历史上最后一个封建王朝，直到 1912 年，被辛亥革命推翻。

第二节　中国近代史（1840—1919 年）

从 1840 年的鸦片战争，到 1949 年的"五四运动"，是中国的近代史时期。

(Jing Nan) and the Northern Han were collectively called the Ten Kingdoms by the *New Five Dynasties History* and the later historians.

The Song Dynasty was from 960 to 1279, and it was the transitional dynasty from the Five Dynasties and Ten Kingdoms to the Yuan Dynasty in the Chinese history. It was divided into two periods, including the Northern Song Dynasty and the Southern Song Dynasty, and there were a total of eighteen emperors, reigning for 319 years.

In 1279 A.D. an ethnic Mongolian Genghis Khan's grandson Kubilai Khan established the Yuan Dynasty, and this was the first dynasty that was ruled by the minority in the Chinese history.

The Italian merchant of Venice Marco Polo came to China, and wrote a book named *Travels of Marco Polo*. It vividly described the status of the Chinese society at that time.

七、The Decline Period of the Feudal Society—the Ming and Qing Dynasties (1368—1840)

In 1368 A. D., Zhu Yuanzhang established the Ming Dynasty.

In 1644, the Manchu established the Qing Dynasty, and this was the last feudal dynasty in the Chinese history. Until 1911, it was overthrown by the Xinhai Revolution (the Revolution of 1911).

Section 2 Early Modern History of China (1840—1919)

It was the Early Modern History period from the Opium War of 1840 to the May Fourth Movement of 1919.

一、鸦片战争（1840 年）

1840 年的鸦片战争，是中国历史的转折点，成为中国近代史的开端。

19 世纪初期，英国向中国秘密输入鸦片，给中国带来了严重的灾难。1939 年，清朝政府派遣官员林则徐去广州禁烟。1840 年，英国政府为了庇护鸦片贸易，武力进攻中国，于是，爆发了鸦片战争。这是第一次鸦片战争。结果，中国战败。1842 年，清朝政府与英国政府签订了《南京条约》，其中有一个条款，就是割让中国香港。

后来，1856 年，又发生了一次鸦片战争，叫作第二次鸦片战争。

二、太平天国革命（1851—1864 年）

1851 年，农民领袖洪秀全领导农民在广西起义，打出了"太平天国"的旗号。1853 年，太平天国定都南京。太平天国革命，是中国历史上规模最大的一次农民革命运动。

1856—1860 年，英法联军向中国发动了第二次鸦片战争，一直打到北京，火烧圆明园。

三、中日甲午战争（1894 年）

1894 年，日本向中国发动了战争，就是中日甲午战争。结果，中国战败。清政府与日本政府签订了《马关条约》，清政府割地赔款。

一、The Opium War (1840)

The Opium War of 1840 was the turning point of the Chinese history, and it became the beginning of the Early Modern History of China.

In the early nineteenth century, England input secretly opium to China, and brought the serious disaster to China. In 1939, the Qing Dynasty government sent the official Lin Zexu to Guangzhou to ban on the opium-smoking and the opium trade. In 1840, the English government attacked China by force in order to shield the opium trade, so the Opium War broke out. This was the First Opium War. As a result, China was defeated. In 1842, the Qing Dynasty government and the British government signed the *Treaty of Nanjing*, and one of the clauses was just to cede the territory Hongkong Island to the British Empire.

Later, in 1856, the Opium War happened once again, and it was called the Second Opium War.

二、The Taiping Revolution (1851—1864)

In 1851, the peasant leader Hong Xiuquan led the peasants to uprise in Guangxi, and hoisted the ensign of the Taiping Heavenly Kingdom. In 1853, the Taiping Heavenly Kingdom built its capital in Nanjing. The revolution of the Taiping Heavenly Kingdom was the biggest farmer revolutionary movement in the Chinese history.

From 1856 to 1860, the British and French allied forces launched the Second Opium War in China, and attacked straight to Beijing, and burnt the Imperial Palace.

三、The Sino–Japanese War of 1894

In 1894, Japan launched the war to China, and this was just the Sino-Japanese War of 1894—1895. As a result, China was defeated. The Qing Dynasty government signed the *Treaty of Maguan* with the Japanese government, and the Qing government ceded territory and paid indemnities.

四、"百日维新"运动

1898 年 6 月 11 日，光绪皇帝颁布诏书，表示变法的决心。从这一天开始，到 9 月 21 日变法失败，历时 103 天，历史上称为"百日维新"运动。这次运动的宗旨是改革封建帝制，学习西方的制度。

1898 年 9 月 21 日，掌握清朝政府权利的慈禧太后（慈禧太后是光绪皇帝的叔母和姨母）下令囚禁了光绪皇帝，变法运动失败。维新运动的主要成员（康有为、谭嗣同、梁启超等人），有的被杀，有的流亡到了国外。

五、义和团运动（1900 年）

1900 年，义和团运动从山东兴起，迅速发展到河北、北京、天津等地区，义和团提出了"扶清灭洋"的口号。英、美、日、俄、德、法、奥、意八个国家组成了八国联军，进行武装干涉。1901 年 9 月，清朝政府与八国政府签订了《辛丑条约》。

六、辛亥革命（1911 年）

1905 年，孙中山在日本建立了中国第一个资产阶级政党——同盟会（辛亥革命后改为国民党）。后来，孙中山把同盟会的纲领概括为三民主义：民族主义，民权主义，民生主义。

四、The One Hundred Days' Reform Movement

On June 11th, 1898, the Emperor Guangxu issued the proclamation and expressed his determination of reform. From this day on, to the failure of the reform on September 21st, the reform lasted for 103 days, and was called the One Hundred Days' Reform Movement. The aim of this movement was to reform the feudal monarchy and learn from the western system.

On September 21st, the Empress Dowager Cixi who mastered the right of the Qing Dynasty government (the Empress Dowager Cixi was the aunt of the Emperor Guangxu) ordered to imprison the Emperor Guangxu, and the reform movement failed. The main members of the reform movement included Kang Youwei, Tan Citong, Liang Qichao and so on. Some were killed, and some fled to the foreign countries.

五、The Boxer Rebellion; the Yihetuan Movement

In 1900, the Boxer Rebellion (the Yihetuan Movement) rose up (sprang up) from the Shandong Province, and developed rapidly to Hebei, Beijing, Tianjin and other areas. It presented the slogan of assisting the Qing Dynasty government and clearing out the foreigners. The eight countries including England, America, Japan, Russia, Germany, France, Austria and Italy formed (constituted) the eight-power allied forces to carry on the armed intervention. In September, 1901, the Qing Dynasty government signed the *Boxer Protocol* with the eight national governments.

六、Xinhai Revolution; the Revolution of 1911; the Chinese Bourgeois Democratic Revolution Led by Dr. Sun Yat-sen

In 1905, Sun Zhongshan set up the first bourgeois party of China in Japan, the Tong Meng Hui, the Chinese Revolutionary League (it was transformed into the Kuomintang after the Revolution of 1911). Later, Dr. Sun Yat-sen summarized the creeds of the Chinese Revolutionary League as the Three People's Principles: Nationalism, Civil Rights (Democracy), and the People's Livelihood.

1911 年 10 月 10 日，同盟会在湖北武昌发动武装起义，获得成功。1912年元旦，中华民国临时政府在南京成立，孙中山就任临时大总统，辛亥革命取得了胜利。

辛亥革命的伟大功绩：推翻了清朝 260 多年的统治，结束了中国两千多年的封建帝制，建立了"中华民国"。

第三节　中国现代史（1919—1949 年）

一、"五四运动"与中国共产党的成立

1919 年 5 月 4 日，中国北京大学的学生发起了"五四运动"，其主要内容是反帝反封建。"五四运动"成为中国近代史与现代史、旧民主主义革命与新民主主义革命的分界线。

1921 年，毛泽东、董必武等一些革命活动家，代表全国各地的共产主义小组，在上海召开了第一次全国代表大会，成立了中国共产党。

二、北伐战争（1926—1927 年）

1924 年，国共两党实现了第一次合作，共同创设了黄埔军校，组织国民革命军。1926 年，国民革命军开始正式向北方进军，讨伐北洋军阀，历史上称为"北伐战争"。

On the tenth of October, 1911, the Chinese Revolutionary League launched the armed uprising in Wuchang, Hubei Province, and achieved success. On the New Year's Day of 1912, the provisional (interim) government of the Republic of China was established in Nanjing, and Dr. Sun Yat-sen assumed the post of the great temporary president. The Revolution of 1911 won victory.

The great merit of the Revolution of 1911 was to have overthrown the rule of more than 260 years of the Qing Dynasty, and ended the Chinese feudal monarchy of more than two thousand years, and built the Republic of China.

Section 3 Modern History of China (1919—1949)

一、The May Fourth Movement and the Establishment of the Communist Party of China

On the fourth of May, 1919, the students of the Peking University in China launched "the May Fourth Movement", and its main contents were to resist the imperialism and the feudalism. The May Fourth Movement became the boundaries both between the Early Modern History and the Modern History of China, and between the Old Democratic Revolution and the New Democratic Revolution.

In 1921, some revolutionary activists including Mao Zedong, Dong Biwu and so on, represented the communist groups all over the country to hold the First National Congress in Shanghai, and set up the Communist Party of China.

二、The Northern Expedition (1926—1927)

In 1924, the two parties, the Communist Party and the Nationalist Party, realized the cooperation for the first time, and jointly created the Huangpu Military Academy, and organized the National Revolutionary Army. In 1926, the National

1925 年，孙中山逝世之后，蒋介石掌握了国民党的领导权。1927 年 4 月，蒋介石发动了反革命政变，并在南京成立了国民政府，大革命失败。这一时期，称为第一次国内革命战争时期。

三、第二次国内革命战争（1927—1937 年）

1927 年 8 月 1 日，中国共产党人周恩来、朱德、贺龙等，在江西南昌发动了武装起义，打响了与国民党进行武装斗争的第一枪。

1927 年 9 月，毛泽东在湖南领导了秋收起义，建立了中国工农红军，开辟了井冈山农村革命根据地。

1934 年 10 月，为了摆脱蒋介石的军事围剿，中国工农红军开始了二万五千里长征。1935 年 10 月，红军到达陕甘宁边区。很快，延安成了全国抗日和革命的中心。

四、抗日战争（1931—1945 年）

中国的抗日战争起始于 1931 年的"九一八事变"。"九一八事变"（又称奉天事变、柳条湖事件）是日本在中国东北蓄意制造并发动的一场侵华事变，是日本帝国主义侵华的开端，也是中国人民抗日战争的开始。

1931 年 9 月 18 日夜，在日本关东军安排下，铁道"守备队"炸毁沈阳柳条湖附近的南满铁路路轨（沙俄修建，后被日本所占），并栽赃嫁祸于中

Revolutionary Army began formally to march to the north to crusade against the Northern Warlords. And this was called the Northern Expedition in the history.

In 1925, after Dr. Sun Yat-sen passed away, Chiang Kai-shek mastered the leadership of the Nationalist Party. In April, 1927, Chiang Kai-shek launched the counterrevolutionary coup, and set up the National Government in Nanjing. The great revolution failed. This period was called the period of the First Revolutionary Civil War.

三、The Second Revolutionary Civil War (1927—1937)

On the first of August, 1927, the Communists Zhou Enlai, Zhu De and He long and so on launched the armed uprising in Nanchang, and fired the first shot of the armed struggle with the Nationalist Party.

In September, 1927, Mao Zedong led the Autumn Harvest Uprising in Hunan Province, and established the Red Army of Workers and Peasants, and opened the Jing Gangshan Rural Revolutionary Base Area.

In October of 1934, in order to get rid of Chiang Kai-shek's military siege, the Chinese Red Army of Workers and Peasants started the 25,000-mile Long March. In October of 1935, the Red Army arrived in the Shaanxi-Gansu-Ningxia Border Region. Soon, Yan'an became the national center of the Anti-Japanese war and revolution.

四、The Anti-Japanese War (1931—1945)

China's war of resistance against Japanese aggression began in 1931 with the September Eighteenth Incident. The September Eighteenth Incident (also known as the Mukden Incident, and the Willow Twig Lake Incident) was one event of aggression against China deliberately created and launched by Japan in the northeast China, the beginning of the Japanese imperialistic invasion of China, and the beginning of the Chinese people's war of resistance against Japanese aggression.

On the night of September eighteenth, 1931, under the arrangement of the Japanese Kwantung Army, the railway garrison blew up the southern Manchuria

国军队。日军以此为借口，炮轰沈阳北大营，这个事件就是"九一八事变"。次日，日军侵占沈阳，又陆续侵占了东北三省。1932年2月，东北全境沦陷。此后，日本在中国东北建立了"伪满洲国"傀儡政权，开始了对东北人民长达14年之久的奴役和殖民统治。

"九一八事变"是日本帝国主义长期以来推行对华侵略扩张政策的必然结果，也是企图把中国变为其独占的殖民地而采取的重要步骤。它同时标志着世界反法西斯战争的开始，揭开了第二次世界大战东方战场的序幕。

1936年12月，发生了"西安事变"。西安事变，又称"双十二事变"。面对日本侵略者的进攻，蒋介石不但不积极抗日，反而提出了"攘外必先安内"的口号。1936年12月12日，张学良和杨虎城将军为了达到劝谏蒋介石改变"攘外必先安内"的既定国策、停止内战、一致抗日的目的，在西安发动"兵谏"，活捉了蒋介石。此后，蒋介石被迫与共产党达成了共同抗日的协议，国共两党实现了第二次合作。

1937年7月7日，日本军队在北京附近的卢沟桥制造了"卢沟桥事变"，抗日战争全面爆发。"卢沟桥事变"又称"七七事变"。1937年7月7日，日军在北平西南卢沟桥附近演习时，夜间日本军队以"己方士兵失踪"为借口，要求进入宛平县城搜查。在遭到"中华民国"驻军拒绝后，日本军队于

railway nearby Willow Twig Lake in Shenyang City (built by the Tsar and later occupied by the Japanese), and incriminated the Chinese army with the planted evidence. The Japanese army used it as an excuse to bombard the North Camp in Shenyang City, and this event was just the September Eighteenth Incident. The next day, the Japanese army invaded and occupied Shenyang City, and then gradually seized the northeastern provinces. In February, 1932, the whole northeastern China fell into the Japanese hands. After that, Japan established the puppet regime of Manchukuo in the northeast China, and began the fourteen years of enslavement and colonial rule to the people of the northeast China.

The September Eighteenth Incident was the inevitable result of the Japanese imperialistic long policy of aggression and expansion against China, and it was also an important step in its attempt to turn China into an exclusive colony. At the same time, it also marked the beginning of the world war against fascism, and opened the prologue of the Second World War in the eastern battlefield.

In December of 1936, the Xi'an Incident happened. The Xi'an Incident is also known as the Double Twelve Incident. Facing the Japanese invasion, Chiang Kai-shek did not actively resist the Japanese, but put forward the slogan that it must first pacify the interior in oder to resist the foreign aggression. On the twelfth of December, 1936, the two generals Zhang Xueliang and Yang Hucheng launched the forced remonstration in Xi'an and captured Chiang Kai-shek alive, in order to achieve their aims to advise Chiang Kai-shek to change the established state policy that it must first pacify the interior to resist the foreign aggression, stop the civil war and unanimously resist Japan. After then, Chiang Kai-shek was forced to reach an agreement with the Communist Party on joint anti-Japanese war, and the two parties, the Nationalist Party and the Communist Party realized the second cooperation. (on the joint fight against Japan)

On the seventh of July, 1937, the Japanese army made the Lu Gou Bridge Incident in the Lu Gou Bridge near Beijing, and the Anti-Japanese War broke out.

The Lu Gou Bridge Incident is also known as the July Seventh Incident. On the seventh of July, 1937, the Japanese army conducted the military exercise nearby the

7月8日凌晨向宛平县城和卢沟桥发动进攻，"中华民国"国军抵抗。驻守在卢沟桥北面的一个连仅余4人生还，余者全部壮烈牺牲。"七七事变"是日本全面侵华开始的标志，是中华民族进行全面抗战的起点，也象征第二次世界大战亚洲区域战事的起始。

1931年7月—1945年8月，中国人民经历了14年的抗日战争。1945年8月，抗日战争胜利。

五、解放战争（1946—1949年）

1946年6月，蒋介石命令他的部队向中国共产党领导的解放区发动全面进攻，于是，中国爆发了第三次国内革命战争，也称为解放战争。

1946—1949年，解放战争进行了三年。1949年10月1日，毛泽东主席在北京天安门城楼上宣告中华人民共和国成立。12月10日，蒋介石逃往台湾省。

第四节　中国当代史（1949年10月至今）

中华人民共和国的成立，是中国近现代史上最重大的事件。

Lu Gou Bridge, southwest of Beiping. In the nighttime, the Japanese army demanded to enter the Wanping County to rummage on the pretext that some of its soldiers were missing. Rejected by the garrison of the Republic of China, the Japanese forces launched an attack on the Wanping County and the Lu Gou Bridge in the early hours of July eighth, and the army of the Republic of China resisted. As a result, the company stationed north of the Lu Gou Bridge had only four lives left, all the rest of which sacrificed their lives bravely and gloriously. The July Seventh Incident marked the beginning of Japan's full-scale invasion of China, and the starting point of China's comprehensive war of resistance, and it also symbolized the start of the regional war in Asia of the World War Two.

From July, 1931 to August, 1945, the Chinese people had experienced the fourteen years of the Anti-Japanese War. In August of 1945, the Anti-Japanese war won (triumphed).

五、The Liberation War (1946—1949)

In June of 1946, Chiang Kai-shek ordered his army to launch the all-out attack (offensive) on the liberated areas under the leadership of the Communist Party. So, the Third Revolutionary Civil War broke out in China, and it was called the Liberation War.

From 1946 to 1949, the Liberation War lasted for three years. On the first of October, 1949, Chairman Mao Zedong declared the founding of the People's Republic of China on the Tian'anmen Rostrum of Beijing. On the tenth of December, Chiang Kai-shek fled to Taiwan Province.

Section 4　Contemporary History of China (Since 1949, 10)

The founding of the People's Republic of China was the most significant event

1978 年 12 月，中共中央召开了十一届三中全会，制定了新的基本路线：以经济建设为中心。

1997 年，中国收回香港。

1999 年，中国收回澳门。

我国现在的目标是：到 2020 年，全面建成"小康社会"。

思考题：

谈谈你对中国历史的认识。

in the neoteric and modern history of China.

In December of 1978, the Central Committee of the Communist Party of China held the Third Plenary Session of the Eleventh Central Committee of the Chinese Communist Party. It formulated the new basic line, taking economic construction as the central task.

In 1997, China took back Hong Kong.

In 1999, China took back Aomen (Macao; Macau).

The current goal of our country is to build a well-off society in an all-round way by 2020.

Thinking question:

Talk about your understanding of China's history.

第三章 中国的人口

中国是世界上人口最多的国家。中国的全国人口普查是每 10 年开展一次。到现在为止，中国已经进行了六次全国人口普查。上一次全国人口普查是在 2010 年。下一次全国人口普查将在 2020 年。

以 2010 年 11 月 1 日零时为标准时点，中国进行了第六次全国人口普查。最新的第六次全国人口普查主要数据显示：中国总人口是 137,053.69 万人。其中：大陆 31 个省、自治区、直辖市及现役军人共有 133,972.49 万人，香港人口是 709.76 万人，澳门人口是 55.23 万人，台湾人口是 2,316.21 万人。

像一切统计数字都值得怀疑一样，人口统计数字也被人怀疑。许多中国主流阶层的人断定，中国现有人口可能已突破 14 亿，甚至已经到了 15 亿了。

Chapter 3   Population of China

China is the most populous nation in the world. China's national population census is conducted once every ten years. So far, China has conducted six national population censuses. The last national population census was held in 2010, and the next national population census will be held in the year 2020.

China carried out the sixth national population census using zero o'clock on the first of November, 2010 as the standard time. The latest main data of the sixth national population census showed that the total population of China was 1.3705369 billion. Among them, the population of the thirty-one provinces, autonomous regions, municipalities directly under the central government and the servicemen on the mainland was altogether 1.3397249 billion, the population of Hong Kong was 7.0976 million, the population of Macao was 552,300, the population of Taiwan was 23.1621 million.

As all statistics are questionable, the population census data are also suspected. Many people of Chinese mainstream classes conclude that the current Chinese population maybe has broken through 1.4 billion, even reached to 1.5 billion.

第一节　中国的人口演变

秦始皇统一中国以前的 2000 多年间，据说，中国人口有 390 万 ~1370 万。

汉朝时期，中国人口有 5,000 万 ~6,000 万。

宋朝时期，中国人口达到 7600 万。

清朝时期，人口迅猛增长。清朝末年，人口达到 4.13 亿。

1949 年，中华人民共和国成立时，人口达到 5.4 亿。

2010 年，中国人口达到 13.7 亿。

从历史可以看出，中国的人口增长有一个明显的特点：台阶式的倍增。第一个台阶是从秦代到西汉，由 1000 万增加到 6000 万。第二个台阶是在清代，在 200 年内，人口由不足 1 亿 增加到 4 亿多。第三个台阶是新中国成立之后，从 1950 年到 2010 年，仅 60 年，就由 5.4 亿增加到了 13.7 亿。预计到 2030 年，中国人口将达到顶峰——16 个亿。

Section 1 Population Evolution of China

It has been said that the Chinese population was 3.9 million to 13.7 million during more than two thousand years before the First Emperor of Qin unified China.

In the period of Han Dynasty, the Chinese population was 50 million to 60 million.

In the period of Song Dynasty, the Chinese population was 76 million.

In the period of Qing Dynasty, the Chinese population increased by leaps and bounds. In the late Qing Dynasty, the population of China reached 413 million.

In the year of 1949, when the PRC was founded, its population was 540 million.

In the year of 2010, the Chinese population has been 1.37 billion.

As can be seen from the history, the China's population growth has an obvious characteristic: the terraced multiplication. The first terrace was from the Qin Dynasty to the Western Han Dynasty, and the population increased from 10 million to 60 million. The second terrace was in the Qing Dynasty, the population increased from less than one hundred million to more than four hundred million within two hundred years. The third terrace was after the PRC was founded, the population increased from 540 million to 1.37 billion within only sixty years, from the year of 1950 to the year of 2010. It is anticipated that China's population will reach the top — 1.6 billion by the year of 2030.

第二节　中国的人口结构

性别结构：男性比例偏高，比女性高 2.53%。

年龄结构：人口老龄化进程逐步加快。

民族结构：少数民族人口增长率高于汉族。

文化结构：中国国民的平均文化水平仍然偏低。

地区结构：中国人口的地区分布极其不平衡——东南部密度大，西北部密度小。人口密度最大的城市是上海。

城乡结构：以前，中国大部分人口是在农村。现在，城镇人口的比例逐年提高。

第三节　中国的计划生育政策

中国为什么要实行计划生育政策呢？因为，中国是一个发展中国家，人口基数过于庞大，而且人口增长过快，已经带来了一系列严重的问题。如果不控制人口的增长，必将造成更加严重的社会问题。因此，从 1980 年开始，中国政府实行了严格的计划生育政策。

Section 2 Demographic Structure of China

Gender Structure:The percentage of males is on the high side, and 2.53% higher than that of females.

Age Structure: The aging process of population is speeding up step by step.

National Structure: The population growth rate of minority is higher than that of the Han ethnic group.

Cultural Structure: The average cultural level of Chinese nationals is still on the low side.

Regional Structure:China's population regional distribution is extremely unbalanced—the population density of the southeast is high, and the population density in the northwest is low. The city whose population density is the biggest is Shanghai.

Urban and Rural Structure: Before, the most population of China was in the countryside. Now, the proportion of urban population is increasing year by year.

Section 3 Birth Control Policy of China

Why has China been implementing the Birth Control Policy? Because China is a developing country, the population base is too big, the population grows too fast, and a series of serious problems have been brought out. If it doesn't control the growth of population, the more serious social problems will surely be caused. Therefore,

中国计划生育政策的基本内容，概括起来，就是八个字：晚婚晚育，少生优生。

晚婚晚育：晚结婚、晚生育孩子。中国的《婚姻法》规定，可以结婚的年龄是，男 22 岁，女 20 岁。那么，比规定年龄推迟三年以上结婚、生孩子，即男子 25 岁、女子 23 岁之后结婚生育，就算晚婚晚育。

少生优生：少生，就是提倡一对夫妇只生育两个孩子；优生，就是提高生育质量，保证婴儿身体健康，智力发达。

思考题：

谈谈对中国人口问题和人口政策的认识。

since 1980, the Chinese government has implemented the strict Birth Control Policy.

The basic contents of China's Birth Control Policy are just eight characters in summary: Later Marriage and Later Childbirth, Fewer Birth and Better Birth.

Later Marriage and Later Childbearing is exactly to marry later and bear a child later. The China's *Marriage Law* stipulates that the age when one person can get married is 22 years old for males, and 20 years old for females. Then, it is Later Marriage and Later Childbearing that one person gets married and bears a child three years later or more than three years later than the stipulated age, which is exactly to get married and bear a child after twenty-five years old for a male, and after twenty-three years old for a female.

Fewer Birth and Better Birth: Fewer Birth is exactly to advocate that a couple should have only two children; better Birth is exactly to increase the quality of birthbearing, and ensure (assure) that the baby will have a healthy body and a developed intelligence.

Thinking Question:

Please talk about your cognition of the problems of the Chinese population and the policy of the Chinese population.

第四章　中国的民族

"中国"这一名称最早出现于西周初期。当时有三个含义：第一，天子所居之城，位于中央，与四方诸侯国相对；第二，周在灭掉商之前，称周人所在的黄河中下游地区为"中原之国"，即"中国"，后来被沿用了下来；第三，夏、商、周时代融为一体的民族以夏为族称，所以，中国又称为"华夏"。

到了春秋战国时代，中原各诸侯国都称自己为"中国"或者"华夏"。

秦始皇统一中国后，还称中国为"九州"，即徐州、冀州、兖州、青州、扬州、荆州、豫州、梁州和雍州。

魏晋时代把"中国"与"华夏"两个词组合起来，称为"中华"。

后来，凡是生活在中华大地上的人，不管是哪族人，都属于"中华民族"。

因为中国人历来把传说之中的黄帝和炎帝作为自己的祖先，所以，中华民族也被称作"炎黄子孙"，但是，一般在正式场合，还是被称作"中华民族"。

Chapter 4 Ethnic Groups of China

China's name first appeared in the early Western Zhou Dynasty. At that time it had the following three meanings. The first one referred to the city where the emperor lived, and it located in the center, opposite the circumambient vassal states (principalities). The second one: Before the Zhou Dynasty exterminated the Shang Dynasty, the middle and lower reaches of the Yellow River Region where the people of the Zhou Dynasty lived were referred to as the Kingdom of the Central Plains, which was namely "China". Later, it has been continued to adopt (use; follow). The third meaning referred to the integrated nation in the Xia, Shang and Zhou Dynasties, taking Xia as the name of the nation, so, China is also called "Huaxia", the ancient name for China. Hua means splendid, or prosperous, or magnificent.

Up to the Spring and Autumn Period and the Warring States Era, every vassal state (principality) called themselves China, or Huaxia.

After the First Emperor of Qin Dynasty unified China, China was still called as the Nine States, a poetic name for China. They were Xuzhou, Jizhou, Yanzhou, Qingzhou, Yangzhou, Jingzhou, Yuzhou, Liangzhou and Yongzhou.

In the eras of Wei and Jin dynasty, the two words "China" and "Huaxia" were integrated, and were called as Zhong Hua.

Later, the people whoever live on the land of China, no matter which ethnic group they belong to, all belong to the Chinese Nation.

Because the Chinese people have always taken the Huang Emperor and the Yan Emperor of the legend as their own ancestors, the Chinese Nation is also called as the Descendants of the Yan and Huang Emperors. But, generally on formal occasions, it is still called the Chinese Nation.

现在的中华民族，包括 56 个民族，其中汉族占全国人口的 91%，55 个少数民族占全国人口的 9%。

第一节　中国的民族状况

一、人口与分布

在中国的 55 个少数民族中，人口在 500 万以上的有 9 个：壮族、满族、回族、苗族、维吾尔族、土家族、彝族、蒙古族和藏族。

壮族主要分布在广西壮族自治区，满族主要分布在东北三省——黑龙江、吉林、辽宁，回族主要分布在宁夏回族自治区，苗族主要分布在贵州省、湖南省和云南省，维吾尔族主要分布在新疆维吾尔自治区，土家族主要分布在湖南省、湖北省和重庆市，彝族主要分布在四川凉山彝族自治州，蒙古族主要分布在内蒙古自治区，藏族主要分布在西藏自治区。

二、语言与文字

中国的 55 个少数民族，几乎都有本民族的语言，但不是每个民族都有

The current Chinese Nation includes 56 ethnic groups, in which the Han ethnic group accounts for 91 percent of the national population, while other 55 minorities account for 9 percent of the national population.

Section 1 Conditions of China's Minorities

一、Population and Distribution

Among the 55 minorities of China, there are 9 minorities whose population is more than five million: the Zhuang ethnic group, the Manchu ethnic group, the Hui ethnic group, the Miao ethnic group, the Uygur ethnic group, the Tujia ethnic group, the Yi ethnic group, the Mongolian ethnic group and the Tibetan ethnic group.

The Zhuang ethnic group is mainly distributed in the Guangxi Zhuang Autonomous Region. The Manchu ethnic group is mainly distributed in three provinces in the northeast of China, including the Province of Helongjiang, the Province of Jilin, and the Province of Liaoning. The Hui ethnic group is mainly distributed in the Ningxia Hui Autonomous Region. The Miao ethnic group is mainly distributed in Guizhou Province, Hunan Province and Yunnan Province. The Uygur ethnic group is mainly distributed in the Xinjiang Uygur Autonomous Region. The Tujia ethinc group is mainly distributed in Hunan Province, Hubei Province and Chongqing. The Yi ethnic group is mainly distributed in the Yi Autonomous Prefecture, Liangshan, Sichuan Province. The Mongolian ethnic group is mainly distributed in the Inner Mongolia Autonomous Region, and the Tibetan ethnic group is mainly distributed in the Tibet Autonomous Region.

二、Languages and Characters

All the 55 minorities of China have almost their native languages, but not every

自己的文字。其中，只有 21 个民族有本民族的文字，其他的 34 个民族，只有本民族的语言，没有本民族的文字。

三、宗教与习俗

中国的少数民族，一般都信仰宗教，包括世界上的三大宗教：伊斯兰教、佛教和基督教。

各个少数民族的风俗习惯很不一样，表现在居住、服饰、饮食、婚丧、嫁娶、节日、娱乐、禁忌等很多方面。

各个民族都有自己的传统节日，比如，傣族的"泼水节"、彝族的"火把节"、藏族的"藏历年"、蒙古族的"那达慕大会"等。

藏族的藏历年与汉族的农历新年大致相同。

蒙古族的那达慕大会："那达慕"是蒙古语的译音，译为"娱乐"或"游戏"。那达慕大会是蒙古族人民的盛会，每年农历六月初四开始，为期五天，也是蒙古族人民喜爱的一种传统体育活动形式。

第二节　中国的民族政策

中国民族政策的一项重要内容就是，实行民族区域自治。

所谓民族区域自治，就是在国家的统一领导下，以少数民族聚居的地

ethnic group has its own characters. Among them, only 21 ethnic groups have their native characters. The other 34 ethnic groups have only their native languages, not their native characters.

三、Religions and Customs

The Chinese minorities generally believe in religions, including the three main religions in the world: Islam, Buddhism and Christianism.

The manners and customs of various ethnic minorities are very different, which are expressed in many aspects, such as residence, apparel (clothing), diet, marriages and funerals, weddings, festivals, recreation, taboos and so on.

Every ethnic group has its own traditional festivals. For example, the Dai ethnic group has the Water-sprinkling Festival, the Yi ethnic group has the Torch Festival, the Tibetan ethnic group has the Tibetan New Year, and the Mongolia ethnic group has the Nadam Fair of the Mongolian people, and so on.

The Tibetan New Year of the Tibet ethnic group is roughly the same as the Lunar New Year of the Han ethnic group.

The Nadam Fair of the Mongolian people: Nadam is the Mongolian transliteration, and it can be translated into "entertainment" or "game". The Nadam Fair is the pageant (the grand meeting, the grand gathering, the distinguished meeting) of the Mongolian people that begins on the fourth of the Lunar June every year and lasts for five days. It is also a favorite traditional sport of the Mongolian people.

Section 2 The Ethnic Policy of China

One important content of the Chinese ethnic policy is exactly to implement the Ethnic Regional Autonomy System.

The so-called Ethnic Regional Autonomy is exactly under the unified leadership

区为基础，设置地方自治政府，让少数民族自己管理本民族自己的地方性事务。

第三节　中国少数民族的发展变化

在七世纪的唐朝时代，为了密切与藏族地区的关系，唐太宗李世民把文成公主嫁给了藏族的首领松赞干布。文成公主带去了纺织、造纸、酿酒、制陶等先进技术，促进了藏族的经济繁荣。

在文化艺术方面，十一世纪之后产生了藏族史诗《格萨尔王传》，柯尔克孜族史诗《玛纳斯》，彝族撒尼人的长篇叙事诗《阿诗玛》等。

著名的三大石窟：甘肃的敦煌石窟、山西大同的云冈石窟、河南洛阳的龙门石窟。

中华人民共和国成立后，少数民族地区发展了现代工业，例如，包头钢铁公司、克拉玛依油田（中华人民共和国成立后开发的第一个大油田）、刘家峡水电站（位于甘肃省）等。

思考题：

谈谈你对中国民族政策的认识。

of the state, on the basis of the concentrated regions of minorities, to set up the local self-government, and let the minorities themselves manage their own local things.

Section 3　Developments and Changes of China's Ethnic Minorities

In the era of the Tang Dynasty in the 7th century, in order to close the relationship with the Tibetan area, the emperor Tang Taizong Li Shimin made the princess Wencheng marry the Tibetan leader Songtsen Gampo. The princess Wencheng brought there the advanced technologies such as the textile process, papermaking, liquor making, pottery and so on, and promoted the economic prosperity of the Tibet.

In culture and art, after the 11th century, there appeared the Tibetan epic of *King Gesar*, the Khalkhas epic of *Manas*, and the long narrative poem *Ashima* of the Sani people, a branch of the Yi ethnic group.

The three most famous grottoes: the Dunhuang Grottoes in Gansu Province, the Datong Yungang Grottoes in Shanxi Province, and the Luoyang Longmen Grottoes in Henan Province.

After the PRC was founded, the modern industry has been developing in the minority area, including the Baotou Iron and Steel Company, the Karamay Oil Field (the first main oil field that was exploited by the PRC), and the Liujiaxia Hydropower Station (in Gansu Province).

Thinking Question:

Talk about your understanding of China's ethnic policy.

第五章　中国的习俗

中国的习俗体现在中国的婚姻家庭，中国的节庆假日和中国的饭菜酒茶之中。

第一节　中国的婚姻家庭

一、婚姻

在封建社会里，中国的婚姻制度是家长包办制度，其特点有三个。

第一，家长（父母）包办。男女双方当事人一直到结婚那一天才见面。

第二，强调"门当户对"。即地位高的人家要找地位高的人家，地位低的人家要找地位低的人家。也就是说，富的找富的，穷的找穷的，否则，就是门不当户不对。

第三，男尊女卑。在中华人民共和国成立之前，男女极不平等，妇女的地位极其低下，存在着买卖婚姻、纳妾、逼婚、抢婚等现象。有金钱、有

Chapter 5   China's Customs

China's customs are embodied in Chinese marriages and families, Chinese festivals and holidays, Chinese foods, dishes, liquors and teas.

Section 1 Chinese Marriages and Families

一、Marriages

In the feudal society, the Chinese marriage system was the system of marriage arranged by parents. It had the following three characteristics.

Firstly, it was arranged by parents. Men and women both parties could not meet until the wedding day.

Secondly, it stressed that the families of the bride and the bridegroom were of equal position in the social scale. It meant that the people of high status should marry with the people from the family of high status, and the people of low status should marry with the persons from the family of low status. That is to say, the rich should marry with the rich, and the poor should marry with the poor. Otherwise, it would not be matched for marriage.

Thirdly, it embodied that men were superior to women. Before the PRC was founded, men and women were extremely unequal, and the status of the women

地位、有势力的男人，可以娶几个老婆，可以妻妾成群。封建帝王更是拥有"三宫""六院""七十二嫔妃"。而女子呢，一旦被丈夫遗弃或者丈夫死去，则必须终身守寡，不能另嫁他人。

中华人民共和国成立后，1950 年 4 月 13 日，颁布了《婚姻法》。1987 年 1 月，又颁布了新的《婚姻法》。强调男女平等、婚姻自由的原则。而且，把结婚年龄从原来的男子 20 岁，女子 18 岁提高到了男子 22 岁，女子 20 岁。

目前，在中国，法律不允许同性恋人结婚。中国的《婚姻法》规定：结婚必须具备以下三个基本条件：第一，结婚必须男女双方完全自愿，不许任何一方对他方加以强迫或任何第三者加以干涉；第二，结婚年龄，男不得早于 22 周岁，女不得早于 20 周岁；第三，必须符合"一夫一妻"的基本原则。

二、家庭

中国的家庭规模，呈现出逐步缩小的趋势。一般情况下，子女结婚之后，与父母分开居住，所以，绝大多数家庭都是夫妻加上孩子的小家庭，那种三代同堂的传统大家庭比例越来越小。

中国的法律规定：子女长大结婚建立了自己的家庭之后，有赡养父母的义务。赡养父母的方式有两种：一种是直接赡养，即父母与子女生活在一起，子女照顾父母的生活，这是一种传统的方式；另一种是间接赡养，即父

was extremely low. And there were the facts of mercenary marriage, concubinage, forced marriage, marriage by capture and so on. The men who had money, status and power could marry several wives, and have a bevy of wives and concubines. The feudal emperors of course had three queens, six yards for women, and seventy-two concubines. But how about women it was? Once she was deserted by her husband or her husband died, then she must be a widow all her life and could not marry another man.

After the PRC was founded, on April 13th, 1950, the *Marriage Law* was enacted. In January 1987, the new *Marriage Law* was enacted. It stresses the principles that men and women are equal and marriage is free. In addition, it changed the ages of marriage from the original twenty years old for men and eighteen years old for women to the twenty-two years old for men and twenty years old for women.

At present, in China, the law does not allow homosexuals to get married. China's *Marriage Law* rules that marriage must meet the following three basic requirements. Firstly, marriage must be based upon complete willingness of both a man and a woman, neither party may use compulsion on the other party, nor third party may interfere. Secondly, about the marriage age: No marriage may be contracted before the man has reached 22 years of age and the woman has reached 20 years of age. Thirdly, the marriage must meet the basic principle of monogamy.

二、Families

The Chinese family scale (household size) has been presenting the gradually narrowing trend. Under normal circumstances, after the sons and daughters get married, they will live separately from their parents. Therefore, the overwhelming majority of families are the small families of a couple with children. The ratio of traditional big families of three generations under one roof is getting smaller and smaller.

Chinese law rules that, after sons and daughters grow up, get married and set up their own families, they have the obligation to support their parents. There are two ways to support their parents. One way is to support parents directly. It means that

母单独居住、生活，但是他们的生活费用由子女提供。

第二节　中国的节庆假日

中国有很多节庆假日，主要包括新年、春节、元宵节、妇女节、清明节、劳动节、青年节、端午节、儿童节、建党节、建军节、中秋节和国庆节等。

一、新年

公历 1 月 1 日，又称元旦。这一天是新一年的开始，全国放假一天。

二、春节

春节的另一名称叫过年，是中国最盛大、最热闹、最重要的一个古老传统节日，也是中国人所独有的节日。

春节是在每年农历的 1 月 1 日（公历 1 月下旬至 2 月中旬之间），也叫旧历年。作为一个节日，它仅指一天，也就是农历的正月初一这一天。作为假期，它有三天假期，再加上前后两个周末，共七天假期。因为这是全中国各个民族都非常重视的传统节日，所以，全国人民连休七天。作为节日活动

parents live together with their sons or daughters, and sons or daughters take care of the life of their parents, and this is a traditonal way. The other way is to support parents indirectly. It means that parents live alone, but their living cost is provided by their sons or daughters. That is to say, sons or daughters should give some money to their parents.

Section 2 Chinese Festivals and Holidays

China has many festivals and holidays, mainly including the New Year, the Spring Festival, the Lantern Festival, the Women's Day, the Tomb-Sweeping Day, the Labor Day, the Youth Day, the Dragon Boat Festival, the Children's Day, the Party's Birthday, the Army Day, the Mid-Autumn Festival and the National Day and so on.

一、The New Year

January 1st of the Gregorian calendar is also called as Yuan Dan [the first daybreak (dawn, day)]. This day is the beginning of the New Year, and the whole nation has one day off.

二、The Spring Festival

The other name of the Spring Festival is Celebrating the New Year, which is the grandest, the most hilarious and the most important ancient traditional festival, also the festival unique to the Chinese.

The Spring Festival is on January 1st of the lunar calendar (between the late January and the mid-February of the Gregorian calendar), and it is called the Lunar New Year. As a festival, it means only one day, namely the first day of the first lunar month. As a holiday, it has three days off, plus two weekends, a total seven-day

和节日气氛，它会持续半个多月，从年三十到正月十五元宵节，都可以说是春节期间。

中国的四个季节：春天在三、四、五三个月，夏天在六、七、八三个月，秋天在九、十、十一三个月，冬天在十二、一、二三个月。正如你所见，中国的春节并不是在春天，而是在冬天，在天气开始转暖的时候。"春节"预示着冬天即将过去，春天快要来临。

关于春节的起源：本来，春节并不叫春节，而是叫作"过年"。据说，过年起源于中国古代（殷商时期）年头岁尾的祭神、祭祖活动，已有4000多年的历史。相传，公元前2000多年的一天，舜即天子位，他带领着部下随员祭拜天地。从此，人们就把这一天当作岁首。据说这就是农历新年的由来，后来叫春节。1911年辛亥革命以后，"中华民国"开始采用公历（阳历）纪年，遂称公历1月1日为"元旦"，称农历正月初一为"春节"。

春节的习俗包括贴红对联、点长明灯、放鞭炮。相传，古时候，有一种凶猛的怪兽叫作"年"。每年到了腊月三十，它就出来到村子里走街串巷，觅食人肉，残害生灵。但是，它非常害怕三种东西：红色、亮光和响声，所

holiday. Because this is the traditional festival that is most valued by all ethnic groups in China, the whole nation has seven days off successively. As to the festival activities and the festival atmosphere, it will last more than half a month, from the lunar December thirtieth to the lunar January fifteenth (the Lantern Festival). This period can be said during the Spring Festival.

The four seasons in China are as follows: Spring includes March, April and May; Summer includes June, July and August; Autumn includes September, October and November; and Winter includes December, January and February. As you see, the Chinese Spring Festival is not in the spring, but in the winter, when the weather begins to warm in winter. The Spring Festival indicates that the winter will be leaving us, and the spring is coming soon.

The origin of the Spring Festival is as follows: Originally, the Spring Festival is called "过年", not the Spring Festival. ("过" means pass, spend or celebrate; "年" means new year; so "过年" means celebrating the new year.) It is said that Celebrating New Year originated from the activities of offering sacrifice to the gods(deities) and ancestors when the old year ended and the new year began in ancient China, and it has had a history of over 4000 years. According to the legend, one day more than 2000 years B.C., Shun (the second chieftain of ancient China) ascended the throne, and he led his subordinates to hold the sacrificial rites to the Heaven and Earth. Since then, people took this day as the beginning of the new year. It is said that this was the origin of the Lunar New Year, and later it has been called the Spring Festival. After the Revolution of 1911, the Republic of China (1912—1949) began to adopt the Gregorian calendar, and it called January 1st of the Gregorian calendar "元旦", and the first day of the first lunar month "春节"。 ("元" means first or primary; "旦" means day, dawn or daybreak. So, Yuan Dan means the first day of the new year of the Gregorian calendar.)

The customs of Chinese Spring Festival include pasting the red antithetical couplets, lighting the ever-burning lamps and setting off firecrackers. According to legend, in ancient times, there was a ferocious monster called Nian. On the lunar

以，人们就用鲜红的对联、明亮的灯光和响亮的鞭炮声来震慑、抵御和驱逐凶猛的怪兽"年"。这就是春节中国人贴红对联、点长明灯和放鞭炮习俗的由来。

春节的前一天，即农历12月30日，叫"除夕"。这一天，全家团圆，吃丰盛的晚餐——"年夜饭"。

吃完年夜饭后，全家围坐欢谈。20世纪80年代以前，整个中国都很贫穷，很多人家里没有电视机。自从电视机普及后，每到除夕晚上，中央电视台以及各省市电视台都要播放春节晚会特别节目，一直到午夜12点以后。有的人看完电视节目后还不休息，一整夜不睡觉，叫作"守岁"。

据传说，中国古代人认为疫病是山鬼闹的，于是就用火烧竹子驱逐山鬼。竹子受热爆开，发出声响，故被称为"爆竹"。后来，放爆竹主要是用来表达人们欢乐的心情。现在，每年到了除夕深夜12点钟，千家万户鞭炮齐鸣，如同暴风骤雨，象征着辞旧岁、迎新春，使春节的热闹气氛达到顶点。

农历1月1日，也叫大年初一。这一天的早晨，北方人家家户户吃饺子，叫"更岁饺子"。南方人吃年糕、汤圆，表示"年年升高""全家团圆"。

December 30th every year, it would come out to some villages to forage for human flesh to eat and slaughter living creatures. But it was very afraid of the three things: the red color, the bright light and the loud noise. Therefore, people used the bright red antithetical couplets, the bright lights and the loud firecrackers to frighten, defense and expel the ferocious monster Nian. This was the origin of the customs of Chinese people's pasting the red antithetical couplets, lighting the all-night lamps and setting off firecrackers when they celebrate the Spring Festival.

The day before the Spring Festival, namely the lunar December 30th, is called the New Year's Eve. On this day, the whole family reunites, and eats the hearty (bumper) supper-the New Year's Eve Dinner (the family reunion dinner).

After having eaten the New Year's Eve Dinner, the whole family sits around and talks merrily. Before the nineteen eighties, the whole of China was very poor, and many people had no television in their homes. Later, since the television became popular, at every New Year's Eve night, the China Central Television Station and all the provincial and municipal television stations will broadcast the Spring Festival Evening Party Special Programs until after twelve o'clock at midnight. Some people will not go to sleep after finishing watching the television programs, even stay up all night, which is called the pernoctation.

According to the legend, the ancient Chinese people thought that the pestilence and lues were made by the goddess (ghost) of the mountain, and then they used the lit bamboo to expel the goddess of the mountain. The bamboo was heated to pop and make noises, therefore this was called "the firecracker" or squib or petard. Later, setting off firecrackers was mainly used to express the happy mood of people. Now, at twelve o'clock at the mid-night of every New Year's Eve , the firecrackers salvo in thousands upon thousands of families, like the hurricane and tempest, indicating to bid farewell to the old year and welcome the new spring, and it makes the lively atmosphere achieve the culmination.

The lunar January 1st is also called the first day of the Lunar New Year. In the morning of this day, every household of the northern people eats the dumplings,

初一以后，人们开始走亲访友，进行"拜年"活动。

三、元宵节

元宵节是在农历正月十五日，也叫"灯节"。这是春节后的第一个月圆之夜。过元宵节，有吃元宵和观灯的习俗。元宵是圆形的，象征着"团圆"。

四、妇女节（三八妇女节）

公历 3 月 8 日，是国际妇女斗争纪念日。1908 年 3 月 8 日，美国芝加哥的妇女们，因为要求男女权利平等而举行示威。次年，在丹麦哥本哈根召开的第二次国际社会主义者妇女大会上，决定将 3 月 8 日这一天作为"国际劳动妇女节"。中国妇女在这一天放假半天。

五、清明节

每年的 4 月 5 日前后是清明节，是扫墓日。这一天，人们一般到亲人和革命烈士的墓前或者纪念碑前扫墓、献花，以示悼念。

called the Changing Year Dumplings. The southern people eat the New Year Cakes and the sweet rice dumpling, indicating the rising year after year and the whole family reunion.

After the first day of the Lunar New Year, people begin to call on their relatives and friends, and carry on the activities of Giving New Year's Greetings.

三、The First Full Moon Festival (the Lantern Festival)

The First Full Moon Festival is on the fifteenth of the first lunar month, and it is also called the Lantern Festival. This is the first night with the full moon after the Spring Festival. When celebrating the Lantern Festival, people have the customs of eating sweet dumplings made of the glutinous rice flour and watching the lanterns. The sweet dumplings are round, to indicate reunion.

四、The Women's Day (the International Working Women's Day on March Eighth)

The eighth of March of the Gregorian calendar is the international women struggle anniversary. On the eighth of March, 1908, the women of Chicago in America held demonstration for equal rights for women to men. In the next year, this day was decided as the International Women's Day at the Second International Socialist Women Conference held in the city Copenhagen, Denmark. The Chinese women have half day off.

五、The Tomb-Sweeping Day

Around April 5th every year is the Clear-and-Bright Festival, namely, the Tomb-Sweeping Day. On this day, people generally go to the front of the graves of their relatives or the monuments (cenotaphs) of the revolutionary martyrs to sweep tombs and present a bouquet in order to denote condolence.

六、劳动节（五一国际劳动节）

公历 5 月 1 日，是全世界劳动人民的节日。1886 年 5 月 1 日，美国芝加哥等地的工人举行罢工和示威游行，反对资本家的残酷剥削，要求实行 8 个小时的工作制度，经过斗争，取得了胜利。

1889 年在巴黎召开的第二国际成立大会，将 5 月 1 日定为"国际劳动节"。中国在这一天全国放假一天。

七、青年节（五四青年节）

青年节是在公历 5 月 4 日。1919 年，在中国的"五四运动"中，青年学生发挥了先锋作用，所以，规定这一天为中国的青年节。

八、端午节

中国的一个重要的传统节日是端午节。端午节是在每年农历的 5 月 5 日，公历 6 月份。

端午节的来历：据说，这个节日是为了纪念中国古代伟大的爱国诗人屈原。屈原是战国时期楚国的大臣。因为他反对楚国的腐败，要求改革，遭到了打击和陷害，并被楚王流放。公元前 287 年，楚国被秦国打败，屈原非常绝望，于该年 5 月 5 日投汨罗江自尽。

六、The Labour Day (the International Labor Day on May 1st)

The first day of May in the Gregorian calendar is the festival of the working people around the world. On May 1st, 1886, the workers of Chicago and other places in America held strikes and demonstrations to oppose the cruel exploitation of the capitalists, and require implementing the work system of eight hours. And through the struggle, they won the victory.

The first day of May was determined to be the International Labour Day at the founding conference of the Second International held in Paris in 1889. China has one day off all over the country on this day.

七、The Youth Day on May 4th

The Youth Day is on May 4th of the Gregorian calendar. In the year 1919, during the May 4th Movement in China, the young students played the vanguard role, therefore, this day was ruled as the Youth Day of China.

八、The Dragon Boat Festival (the 5th day of the 5th lunar month)

There is another traditional festival in China—Dragon Boat Festival. Dragon Boat Festival is on the fifth day of the fifth lunar month, in June of the Gregorian calendar.

The origin of the Dragon Boat Festival is as follows: It is said that this festival is to commemorate the great patriotic poet Qu Yuan in ancient China. Qu Yuan was a minister of Chu State during the Warring States Period. Because Qu Yuan opposed the corruption of the Chu State and required (requested) reformation, he was hit and framed, and was exiled by the king of the Chu State. In the year 287 B.C., the Chu State was defeated by the Qin State, Qu Yuan was very despairing , and committed suicide by drowning himself in the Miluo River on May 5th of that year.

端午节的习俗之一：赛龙舟。据传说，屈原投汨罗江之后，江边的百姓纷纷怀着沉痛的心情，划着小船打捞屈原的尸体。后来，每年到了这一天，人们就要在江河上划龙舟，以表示对屈原的悼念。后来，划龙舟（赛龙舟）就变成了民间的一项体育竞赛活动。

在中国，南方方言与北方方言有很大的不同。一些赛龙舟的歌曲是南方方言，主要是潮州和汕头方言，即潮汕方言。一般情况下，北方人都很难听懂这些歌曲的歌词。

端午节的习俗之二：吃粽子。据说，端午节吃粽子也与屈原有关。屈原投江死后，每年到了 5 月 5 日，人们就用竹筒装上大米投入江中祭祀他。后来，人们用竹叶包上糯米做成粽子投入江中来纪念屈原。现在，粽子成了这一节日的传统食品。

九、儿童节（六一儿童节）

儿童节是在公历 6 月 1 日，是全世界儿童的节日。1949 年，国际民主妇女联合会为了保护全世界儿童的权益，在莫斯科举行的会议上，决定将 6 月 1 日定为国际儿童节。

十、建党节（七一建党节）

建党节是在公历 7 月 1 日。1921 年 7 月 1 日，中国共产党在上海成立。1941 年决定将 7 月 1 日作为中国共产党的诞生日。

One of the customs of Dragon Boat Festival is Dragon Boat Racing. According to the legend, after Qu Yuan jumped into the river , the people with the heavy and grieved heart on the both sides of the river paddled small boats one after another to salvage the corpse of Qu Yuan. Later, on this day every year, people would paddle the Dragon Boat on the streams and rivers to express their mourning for Qu Yuan. Still later, the dragon-boat racing became the folk sports competition activities.

In China, the southern dialects are very different from the northern dialects. Some songs about Dragon Boat Racing are in the southern dialects, mainly the dialects of Chaozhou and Shantou, namely the Chaoshan dialects. Generally, the northerners cannot understand the lyrics of these songs.

The second custom of the Dragon Boat Festival is to eat the traditional Chinese rice-puddings (the glutinous rice dumplings) . According to the legend, it is also associated with Qu Yuan to eat the rice-puddings around the Dragon Boat Festival. After Qu Yuan died, on the fifth day of the fifth lunar month every year, people would fill the bamboo tubes with the rice and cast them into the river to sacrifice to him. Later, people used the bamboo leaves to package up the glutinous rice to make the rice-puddings and throw them into the river to commemorate Qu Yuan. Now, the rice-puddings have become the traditional food of the festival.

九、The Children's Day

The Children's Day is on June 1st of Gregorian calendar, and this is the festival for the children all over the world. In the year of 1949, the Women's International Democratic Federation, in order to protect the rights of children around the world, decided at the meeting held in Moscow that the first day of June was the International Children's Day.

十、The Party's Birthday

The Party's Day is on July 1st of Gregorian calendar. On July 1st, 1921, the Communist Party of China was founded in Shanghai. In the year of 1941, the first

十一、建军节（八一建军节）

建军节是在公历 8 月 1 日。1927 年 8 月 1 日，中国共产党的领导人周恩来、朱德、贺龙、叶挺等人在江西南昌发动了武装起义，因此，后来把这一天定为了建军节。

十二、中秋节

中国还有一个重要的传统节日——中秋节。中秋节是在每年的农历 8 月 15 日，约公历 9 月。这一天居秋季的中间，所以被称为中秋节，全国放假一天。中秋节的习俗是吃月饼和赏月，全家人团圆欢聚。

如果天气晴朗，在中秋节的晚上，天空中的月亮是一年中最圆的。在中国传统文化里，圆满的月亮象征着家庭的团圆和美满的生活。因此，中国人庆祝这个节日的主要方式就是所有的家庭成员聚集在家里吃团圆饭、月饼和赏月。圆形的月饼和圆满的月亮有着同样的意义。

中秋节的由来：相传远古的时候，天上有 10 个太阳同时出现，晒得庄稼枯死，民不聊生。一个名叫后羿的英雄，力大无穷。他同情受苦的百姓，于是登上昆仑山顶，拉开神弓，一气射下 9 个太阳，并严令最后一个太阳按时起落。从此，他受到百姓的爱戴。

day of July was decided to be the birthday of the Communist Party of China.

十一、The Army Day

The Army Day is on the first day of August of Gregorian calendar. On the first day of August, 1927, the leaders of the Communist Party of China including Zhou Enlai, Zhu De, He Long and Ye Ting and so on, launched an armed uprising in Nanchang City, Jiangxi Province. Later, this day was ruled as the Army Day.

十二、The Mid-Autumn Festival (15th day of the 8th lunar month)

China has still an important traditional festival——the Mid-Autumn Festival. The Mid-Autumn Festival is on August 15th of the lunar calendar every year, in about September of the Gregorian calendar. This day is in the middle of the Autumn, therefore, it is called as the Mid-Autumn Festival. People have one day off for this festival.The customs of the Mid-Autumn Festival include to eat mooncakes and to enjoy the glorious full moon, showing the happy reunion and get-together of the whole family.

In the evening of the Mid-Autumn Festival the moon in the sky is the roundest during the whole year, if the weather is clear. In our traditional Chinese culture, the round moon symbolizes the family reunion and a satisfactory life. So, the main fashions by which Chinese people celebrate the festival are that all the family members gather at home to eat family reunion dinner and appreciate the round moon. Of course, on this day, all the Chinese people will eat moon cakes. The round moon cakes have the same sense as the round moon.

The origin of the Mid-Autumn Festival is as follows: According to the legend, in the time immemorial, there were ten suns appearing in the sky at the same time, and they tanned the crops to death and made the masses have no means to live. There was a hero named Hou Yi, and he was very mighty. He had sympathy for the people who were suffering, so he climbed the top of Mountain Kunlun, pulled the god bow,

一天，后羿巧遇王母娘娘，并求得一包不死药。只要吃下此药，就能即刻升天成仙。后羿不忍独自成仙，便把不死药交给妻子嫦娥珍藏，不料被心术不正的蓬蒙看见了。蓬蒙趁后羿外出的时候，手持宝剑闯入后羿家的内宅，威逼嫦娥交出不死药。情急之下，嫦娥将不死药一口吞下。当即她飘离地面，飞上天去。由于嫦娥牵挂着丈夫，便飞到离人间最近的月亮上成了仙。

后羿回来以后，悲痛欲绝，仰望着夜空，呼唤着爱妻的名字。这时候，他惊奇地发现，天空中的月亮格外皎洁明亮——因为这一天是阴历的 8 月 15 日，而且有个晃动的身影酷似嫦娥。后羿思念妻子，只好摆上香案，放上蜜食鲜果，遥寄在月宫里眷恋着自己的嫦娥。从此，百姓纷纷在月下摆设香案，向善良的嫦娥祈求吉祥平安。

中秋节吃月饼的由来：据说，中秋节吃月饼始于元代。当时朱元璋领导汉族人民反抗元朝暴政，约定在 8 月 15 日这一天起义，并以互赠月饼的方法把字条夹在月饼中间传递消息。从此，中秋节吃月饼的习俗便在民间传播开来。

and shot down nine suns at one go, and then ordered strictly the last sun to rise and set on time. Since then, he was loved by the people.

One day, Hou Yi encountered the Queen Mother, and got a pack of immortal medicine. As long as he ate this medicine, he would be able to fly to the sky and become an immortal at once. Hou Yi could not bear to become an immortal alone, so he gave the immortal medicine to his wife Chang'e and made her treasure it. Unexpectedly, this was seen by Peng Meng who harbored the evil intentions. When Hou Yi went out, Peng Meng broke into the inner chambers of Hou Yi's home with a sword in his hand, and bullied Chang'e to surrender the immortal medicine. In a moment of desperation, Chang'e swallowed the immortal medicine at one stroke. She immediately floated off the ground and flew to the sky. Because Chang'e worried about her husband, she flew to the moon that was the closest to the human society and became an immortal.

After Hou Yi came home, he was so grieved that he was not about to live. He looked up at the night sky calling for his loved wife's name. At that time, he was surprised to find that the moon in the sky was extraordinary clear and bright—because this day was the 15th day of August in the lunar calendar, and there was a shaking shadow resembling Chang'e very much. Hou Yi missed his wife very much, then he set the incense table, and put the honey food and fresh fruit on it, and held a memorial ceremony for Chang'e who was sentimentally attached to him in the moon palace. Since then the people began to set the incense table under the moon one after another, and prayed to kind Chang'e for peace and prosperity.

The origin of eating moon cakes in the Mid-Autumn Festival is as follows: Reputedly, the custom of eating moon cakes in the Mid-Autumn Festival began in the Yuan Dynasty. At that time, there was a peasant uprising leader named Zhu Yuanzhang. He led the Han people against the tyranny of the Yuan Dynasty, and appointed to uprise on the day of August 15th. People put the notes in the moon cakes to convey news using the method of exchanging moon cakes. Since then, the custom of eating moon cakes in the Mid-Autumn Festival has been spread in the folk.

月饼发展到今天，品种更加繁多，风味因地各异。其中京式、苏式、广式、潮式等月饼广为我国南北各地的人们所喜爱。

十三、国庆节（十一国庆节）

中国的国庆节是在公历 10 月 1 日，这一天是中华人民共和国成立之日。1949 年 10 月 1 日，在北京的天安门城楼上，中华人民共和国主席毛泽东庄严地向全世界宣告：中华人民共和国成立了。此后，每年到了 10 月 1 日这一天，中国人民都要进行庆祝。

此外，全国性的节日还有：

教师节：公历 9 月 10 日；

重阳节：农历 9 月 9 日。

此外，少数民族的节日有：

广西壮族的歌圩节：农历 3 月 3 日；

云南傣族的泼水节：清明节前后；

藏族的藏历年：3 月；

彝族的火把节：农历 6 月 20 日起三天；

瑶族的达努节：农历 5 月 29 日；

蒙古族的那达慕大会：8、9 月；

伊斯兰教的回族、维吾尔族、哈萨克族的古尔邦节：12 月。

As the moon cakes develop to today, its varieties are more diverse, and its flavors are very different from place to place. Among them, the Beijing-style moon cake, Suzhou-style moon cake, Guangzhou-style moon cake, Chaozhou-style moon cake and so on are widely loved by the people all over the north and south in our country.

十三、The National Day

The National Day of China is on the first day of October in Gregorian calendar, and this day is the founding day of the People's Republic of China. On the first day of October in 1949, on the city gate tower of Tian An Men of Beijing, Mao Zedong, the Chairman of the People's Republic of China, declared solemnly to the whole world that the People's Republic of China had been founded. Since then, this day is celebrated by the Chinese people every year.

Besides these above festivals, the nationwide festivals still include:

The Teachers' Day is on September 10th, the Gregorian calendar;

The Double Ninth Festival is on the ninth day of the ninth lunar month.

Besides these nationwide festivals, the festivals for the ethnic minorities are as follows.

The Singing Fair Festival of Guangxi Zhuang ethnic group is on the third day of the third lunar month.

The Water-Splashing Festival of Yunnan Dai ethnic group is around (before or after) the Tomb-sweeping Festival.

The Tibetan New Year of the Tibetan ethnic group is in March.

The Torch Festival of Yi ethnic group is the three days from the twentieth day of the sixth lunar month.

The Danu Festival of Yao ethnic group is on the twenty-ninth day of the fifth lunar month.

The Nadam Fair of the Mongolian People is in August or September.

The Corban Festival of the Hui ethnic group of Islam, the Uygur ethnic group and the Kazak ethnic group is in December.

第三节 中国的饭菜酒茶

中国的饭菜酒茶品种丰富，花样繁多，风味各异。

一、饭菜

中国人的主食，以大米和面粉为主。南方人喜欢吃大米及用米粉做的食物，比如米线、年糕等。北方人喜欢吃面食，比如馒头、烙饼、包子、花卷、面条、饺子等。中国人的副食以猪、牛、羊、鸡、鸭、鱼肉，以及蔬菜、豆制品等为主。一般有"南甜北咸、东酸西辣"的说法，即南方人喜欢吃甜的，北方人喜欢吃咸的，山西人喜欢吃酸醋，四川人喜欢吃辣椒。

中国的饭菜风味，可以分为四大菜系：黄河中下游的山东菜系，长江上游的四川菜系，长江中下游以及东南沿海的江苏、浙江菜系（江浙菜系），珠江以及南方沿海的广东菜系。

更细致地区分，还可以分为八大菜系：山东菜、湖南菜、四川菜、福建菜、广东菜、江苏菜、浙江菜、安徽菜。

Section 3 Chinese Foods Dishes Liquors and Teas

China's foods, dishes, liquors and teas are rich in varieties and flavors.

一、Foods and Dishes

The staples of the Chinese people are dominated by rice and flour. The southern people like to eat cooked rice and something made of rice flour, such as steamed rice, and New Year Cake and so on. The northern people like to eat the cooked wheaten food, such as steamed bun, baked pancake, steamed stuffed bun, steamed twisted roll, noodle and dumpling and so on. The subsidiary food of the Chinese people are dominated by pork, beef, mutton, chicken, duck, fish, vegetables and bean products, etc. Generally, there is a saying that the south food is sweet, the north food is salty, the east food is sour (acid), and the west food is spicy. Namely, the southerners like to eat the sweet, the northerners like to eat the salty, the easterners like to eat the sour vinegar, and the westerners like to eat the pungent chilies (peppers).

According to the flavour (relish, taste), Chinese dishes can be divided into the four major cuisines including the Shandong Cuisine in the middle and lower reaches of the Yellow River, the Sichuan Cuisine in the upper reaches of the Yangtze River, the Jiang Zhe Cuisine in the middle and lower reaches of the Yangtze River and the south-east coastal areas, and the Guangdong Cuisine in the Pearl River Basin and the south coast.

The Chinese cuisines can meticulously (in greater details) be divided into the eight major cuisines including the Shandong Cuisine, the Hunan Cuisine, the Sichuan Cuisine, the Fujian Cuisine, the Guangdong Cuisine, the Jiangsu Cuisine, the Zhejiang Cuisine, and the Anhui Cuisine.

山东菜的味道比较咸：泰山的干炸红鳞鱼，糖醋鲤鱼，德州的脱骨扒鸡，青岛的油爆海螺、炸蛎黄。

四川菜的特点是麻辣味浓厚：鱼香肉丝、宫保鸡丁、干烧鲫鱼、清汤银耳、肉末豆腐、麻婆豆腐。

江浙菜以煮炖焖煨的做法为特长，调味少，强调原材料的本来味道，浓淡相宜，甜味较多：鸭包鱼翅、扒烧整猪头、水晶肴肉、清蒸鲥鱼、西湖醋鱼。

广东菜以煎、炸、烧、烩为主，强调鲜嫩爽滑。最为有名的是蛇菜"龙虎斗"。它的主要原料是三种蛇和貉，配上二十几种调料，经过几十道工序做成，是兽肉菜中最高级的，具有极高的营养价值。

北京名菜：北京烤鸭，涮羊肉。

二、酒茶

据说，中国是从夏朝开始造酒的。中国的传统酒主要是白酒，酒性浓烈，一般都在五六十度，近年来也有三四十度的。

中国的十大名酒：指贵州茅台、五粮液、洋河大曲、泸州老窖、汾酒、

The flavour of Shandong dishes is more salty: the Dry Fried Red Phosphorus Fish of Mountain Tai, the Fried Carp with Sweet and Sour Sauce, the Braised Chicken off Bone of Dezhou, the Sautéed Conch Slices and the Deep-Fried Oysters of Qing Dao.

The characteristic of the Sichuan dishes is thick spicy, such as the Fish Flavored Pork Slices (Shredded Pork with Garlic Sauce), Sauted Chicken Cubes with Chillies and Peanuts (Spicy Diced Chicken with Peanuts), Dry Braised Crucian Carp, Consomme with White Fungus, Bean Curd with Minced Meat, and Stewed Bean Curd with Minced Meat in Pepper Sauce.

The dishes of Jiangsu and Zhejiang provinces take the practice of boiling, simmering, stewing and braising for specialties, and the seasoning is less, emphasizing the original taste of raw materials. Its richness and leanness is suitable, and the sweet taste is more. Duck Color Shark's Fin, Braised Whole Pig Head, Salted Pork in Jelly, Steamed Shad, and West Lake Fish in Vinegar Gravy.

The Guangdong dishes are dominated by frying, deep-frying, stewing and braising, and emphasize freshness and smoothness. The most famous dish is the snake dish "Dragon and Tiger Fight". Its main materials are the three kinds of snakes and racoon dog, matched with more than twenty kinds of flavours, and it is made after dozens of working procedures. And it is the highest dish with a very high nutritional value among the animal meat dishes.

The famous dishes of Beijing : Beijing Roast Duck, and Instant-boiled Mutton (Mutton Slices Cooked in Hot Pot).

二、Liquors and Teas

It is said that China began to make liquor in the Xia Dynasty. The traditional Chinese liquor is mainly the white spirit, and its alcoholic strength is strong, generally fifty or sixty degrees. In recent years, there are also some white spirits in thirty or fourty degrees.

China's top ten famous white spirits refer to Guizhou Maotai, Five Grain

郎酒、古井贡酒、西凤酒、贵州董酒、剑南春十大白酒品牌。

中国十大名酒品牌
贵州茅台
五粮液
洋河大曲
泸州老窖
汾酒
郎酒
古井贡酒
西凤酒
贵州董酒
剑南春

中国是世界上第一个生产茶叶的国家，被称作"茶叶的故乡"。

中国的茶叶可以分为五大类：花茶、绿茶、红茶、乌龙茶、紧压茶。

中国的十大名茶：杭州的龙井茶、苏州的茉莉花茶、太湖洞庭山的碧螺春、福建安溪的铁观音、安徽黄山的黄山毛峰、福建武夷山的武夷岩茶、安徽祁门的祁门红茶、河南信阳的信阳毛尖、贵州都匀的都匀毛尖、安徽齐云山的六安瓜片。

中国人的饮茶习惯：北方人喜欢喝花茶，特别是茉莉花茶；江浙、上海

Liquid, Yanghe Big Yeast, Luzhou Old Cellar, Fen Liquor, Lang Liquor, Gujinggong Liquor, Xifeng Liquor, Guizhou Dong Liquor and Jiannanchun Liquor. These are the top ten famous brands of Chinese white spirits.

English Interpretation on the Brands of China's Top Ten Famous White Spirits
贵 :expensive; 州 :state; 茅 :ramie; cogongrass; 台 :platform; stage; stand; table
五 :five; 粮 : grain; 液 :fluid; liquid
洋 :ocean; foreign; modern; vast; silver coin; 河 :river; 大 :big; 曲 :bent; twist wrong; song; tune; music; leaven; yeast
泸 :character used for place name; 州 :state; 老 :old; 窖 :cellar
汾:The name of a river, Fenhe River, 716 kilometers long, in central Shanxi Province, the second largest tributary of the Yellow River
郎 :man; my darling; an ancient official title
古 :old; age-old; ancient; paleo; palae; 井 :well; orderly; 贡 :tribute
西 :west; 凤 :phoenix
贵 :expensive; 州 :state; 董 :a surname; director; trustee
剑 :sword; 南 : south; 春 :spring

China was the first country that produced tea in the world, which is called as the hometown of tea.

The Chinese tea can be divided into five types, including Flowering Tea, Green Tea, Black Tea, Oolong Tea and Compressed Tea.

China's top ten famous teas: Dragon Well Tea of Hangzhou, Jasmine Tea of Suzhou, Blue Spiral Spring of the Cave Courtyard Mountain in Tai Lake, Iron (Buddhism) Goddess (Avalokitesvara) Tea of Anxi in Fujian Province, Yellow Mountain Fuzz Tip from the Yellow Mountain in Anhui Province, Wuyi Rock Tea from the Wuyi Mountain of Fujian Province, Qimen Black Tea from the Qimen County of Anhui Province, Xinyang Fuzz Tip Tea from Xinyang of Henan Province, Duyun Fuzz Tip Tea from Duyun of Guizhou Province, and Liu'an Melon Seed Tea from the Qiyun Mountain of An'hui Province.

The Chinese habit of tea drinking is as follows: the northerners like to drink

人喜欢喝绿茶，特别是龙井、毛峰和碧螺春；广东人喜欢喝红茶，特别是祁门红茶。

中国的茶具一般是：一个茶壶、四个茶碗和一个茶盘，这称作一套茶具。

著名的茶具有：江西景德镇的陶瓷、河北省邯郸磁州窑的陶器，还有江苏宜兴的紫砂壶。

思考题：

谈谈你对中国习俗的体验和认识。

the Scented Tea, especially the Jasmine Tea; the people from Jiangsu and Zhejiang provinces and Shanghai City like to drink the Green Tea, especially the Dragon Well Tea, the Fuzz Tip Tea and the Blue Spiral Spring Tea; and the people of Guangdong Province like to drink the Black Tea, especially the Qimen Black Tea.

The Chinese tea set generally consists of a tea pot, four tea bowls and a tea tray, and they are called as a tea set.

The famous tea sets are the ceramic of Jingdezhen in Jiangxi Province, the pottery of the Magnetic State Kiln in Handan City, Hebei Province, and the dark-red enamelled pottery (teapot) of Yixing, Jiangsu Province.

Thinking Question:

Talk about your experiences and understanding of Chinese customs.

第六章　中国的艺术

艺术是一个内容广泛的概念，它包括书法、绘画、音乐、舞蹈、戏剧、电影、曲艺（曲艺是中国民间艺术形式，包括民谣、评书、快板儿、相声等）、建筑、雕塑、杂技等。

第一节　中国的书法·绘画

一、书法

书法是汉字的书写艺术。汉字的书写，为什么会成为一门艺术呢？因为世界上的其他文字，都是表音文字，而汉字是表意文字，是象形方块字，具有其他文字所没有的审美价值。

中国书法艺术的历史，也就是汉字的历史。中国汉字的发展，大体经历了以下几个阶段：甲骨文、金文、篆书、隶书、草书、楷书、行书。

三千多年之前出现的甲骨文笔画又细又硬，字形又瘦又长，给人的感觉是硬挺而古朴，是中国最早的书法。

Chapter 6   Chinese Arts

Art is a concept whose content is broad, and it includes calligraphy, painting, music, dancing, drama, movie and Quyi (Quyi is the Chinese folk art forms, including ballad singing, story telling, clapper talks, cross talks, comic dialogues, etc.), architecture, sculpture, acrobatics and so on.

Section 1 Chinese Calligraphy and Painting

一、Calligraphy

Calligraphy is the writing art of the Chinese characters. Why has the writing of Chinese characters become an art？Because the other characters in the world are all phonography languages, while Chinese characters are the ideograph, the pictograph, and have the aesthetic value that the others don't have.

The history of Chinese calligraphy art, is also the history of Chinese characters. The development of Chinese characters has roughly experienced following stages: Inscription on Bones or Tortoise Shells of the Shang Dynasty, Inscription on Ancient Bronze Objects, Seal Character, Official Script, Cursive Script, Regular Script and Running Script.

More than three thousand years ago, there appeared the Inscription on Bones. The strokes were both thin and hard, and the fonts were slim, which gave people a

商周时期，文字主要铸在青铜器上，而那个时候称"铜"为"金"，所以，这个时期的文字又叫作"金文"。青铜器又以钟与鼎居多，所以又叫作"钟鼎文"。金文的笔画比甲骨文粗壮，线条比甲骨文流畅，它表现出一种庄严敦厚的风格，具有相当强的艺术性。

春秋战国时代，秦国的文字叫作"大篆"。

秦始皇统一六国后，形成的文字叫作"小篆"。它的轮廓是基本整齐的长方形，标志着汉字已经进入了比较成熟的时期。大篆和小篆统称作"篆书"。

秦代，还出现了一种新的字体——"隶书"。因为这种字体是在处理有关徒隶（罪犯）时所用，写得简单草率，所以叫作"隶书"。到了西汉中期，隶书成为社会通行的正式字体。它的整个轮廓呈扁形，给人以端庄安稳的感觉。

就在隶书发展的同时，还出现了一种新的字体"草书"。草书，就是"隶书"的潦草写法。其特点是：写得潦草、快速，笔画与笔画勾连，字与字勾连，字的形状高度简化，有时甚至只有个大概的轮廓。

sense that is stiff and of primitive simplicity. And this was the earliest calligraphy in China.

In the period of Shang and Zhou Dynasties, the characters were mainly cast on bronzes, and at that time people called copper as gold, so the characters of this period were called "Jinwen" (the Gold Characters) — Inscription on Ancient Bronze Objects. At that time, most of the bronzes were bells and pots, so it was also called as the Inscription on Ancient Bells and Cauldrons. The strokes of the Inscription on Ancient Bronze Objects were thicker and stronger than the Inscription on Bones or Tortoise Shells of the Shang Dynasty, and the lines were smoother than that of the Inscription on Bones or Tortoise Shells of the Shang Dynasty. It showed a solemn and gentle style, and had quite a strong artistic quality.

In the eras of the Spring and Autumn Period and the Warring States Period, the characters of Qin State were called the Big-seal Script.

After the First Emperor of Qin Dynasty unified the six states, the characters were formed to be called as the Small-seal Script. Its outline was the basically neat rectangle, which marked that the Chinese characters had entered a more mature period. The Big-seal Script and the Small-seal Script are called by a joint name, the Seal Character.

In the Qin Dynasty, there still appeared a new kind of font — the Official Script. Because this kind of font was used to deal with the files about the criminals, written simply and hastily, it was called as the Official Script. Up to the mid Western Han Dynasty, the Official Script became the official font that prevailed in the society. Its whole outline (entire contour) presented a flate shape, and gave people the sense of dignity and security.

As the Official Script was developing, there still appeared a new kind of font — "Cursive Script". The Cursive Script is exactly the cursive writing way of the Official Script. Its characteristics are that it is written cursively (perfunctorily) and apace (fleetly), the strokes are linked together, the characters are connected with each other, and the shape is simplified drastically, sometimes even only a rough profile can be recognized.

魏晋南北朝时期，形成"楷书"。整个字体的形态由隶书的扁形变成了方形，从而第一次使得中国的汉字变成了方块字。到隋唐时期，楷书字体基本成熟，成为最主要的字体。

晋代，还出现了另外一种书法——行书。它介于楷书与草书之间，比楷书随便，可以写得比较快，但又不是快得潦草难认。行书既美观大方，又方便实用。

中国古代杰出的书法家有晋代的王羲之、王献之父子，唐代的张旭、怀素、颜真卿、柳公权、欧阳询，宋代的苏东坡、黄庭坚，元代的赵孟頫，明代的董其昌、张瑞图，清代的郑板桥、吴昌硕等。

中国的三大碑林——孔庙碑林、西安碑林、昭陵碑林，集中了大量的石碑。石刻碑文是我国古代书法艺术的宝库。昭陵，是唐太宗李世民的陵墓，位于咸阳市礼泉县九嵕（zōng同"崰"）山，是关中"唐十八陵"中规模最大的一座。

中国现代著名的书法家有赵朴初、刘海粟、陈叔亮、启功、黄苗子。

二、绘画

战国时期，楚墓的帛画《龙凤人物图》《御龙人物图》具有很高的艺术水平。

In the period of Wei, Jin, Southern and Northern Dynasties, the Regular Script was formed. The shape of the whole font turned into the square shape from the flate shape of the Official Script, and thus it made Chinese characters become the square-shaped characters for the first time. Up to the periods of Sui and Tang Dynasties, the font of the Regular Script was basically mature, and changed to be the overriding font.

In the Jin Dynasty, there still appeared another kind of calligraphy — the Running Script. It is between the Regular Script and the Cursive Script, more casual than the Regular Script, and can be written faster, but not so fast as to be hard to be recognized. And it is both beautiful and easy, also convenient and practical.

The outstanding calligraphers in Ancient China included: the father and son of Jin Dynasty: Wang Xizhi and Wang Xianzhi, Zhang Xu, Huai Su, Yan Zhenqing, Liu Gongquan, Ouyang Xun of Tang Dynasty, Su Dongpo, Huang Tingjian of Song Dynasty, Zhao Mengfu of Yuan Dynasty, Dong Qichang, Zhang Ruitu of Ming Dynasty, Zheng Banqiao and Wu Changshuo of Qing Dynasty and so on.

China's three big forests of steles include the Confucius Temple Forest of Steles, the Xi'an Forest of Steles, and Zhaoling Mausoleum Forest of Steles, in which a lot of stone tablets are concentrated. The inscription on the stone tablets is the treasure house of the ancient calligraphy art in our country. The Zhao (clear, obvious, manifest) Mausoleum is the mausoleum of the Emperor Tang Taizong Li Shimin, located in the Mountain Jiu Zong, Liquan County, Xianyang City, the largest one among the eighteen mausoleums of the Tang Dynasty in Guanzhong Region (the Central Shaanxi Plain).

The famous calligraphers in Modern China are Zhao Puchu, Liu Haisu, Chen Shuliang, Qi Gong and Huang Miaozi.

二、Painting

The paintings on silk of Chu tombs of the Warring States Period, *Dragon and Phoenix Figure Painting*, *Imperial Dragon Figure Painting* had a high artistic level.

秦汉时期，汉代的帛画和壁画，精彩动人。

魏晋南北朝时期，敦煌壁画有很高的艺术欣赏价值。

这一时期的著名画家有顾恺之、曹不兴、戴逵、陆探微和卫协。

从隋唐到宋代，唐朝壁画占主要地位。隋朝展子虔的《游春图》，是现存最早的山水画作品。宋代张择端的《清明上河图》，是一幅社会风俗画。

这一时期的著名画家有：展子虔、阎立本、尉迟乙僧、吴道子、李思训、王维、张萱、周昉、张择端、董源、范宽、刘松年、马远、赵昌等。

元朝时期，山水花鸟画成就突出。著名的画家有元四家：黄公望、王蒙、倪瓒、吴镇。

明代的著名画家有：浙派画家戴进；苏州吴门画派沈周、文徵明、唐寅、仇英；写意花鸟画派徐渭；工笔花鸟画派边景昭、吕纪。

清代的著名画家有：四大画僧弘仁、髡残、石涛、朱耷；扬州八怪郑板桥、罗聘、黄慎、李方膺、高翔、金农、李鱓、汪士慎；上海画派任伯年、吴昌硕。

中国现代著名画家：齐白石（虾），徐悲鸿（马），潘天寿（鹰），黄宾虹（山水），李苦禅（花鸟），李可染（山水），王雪涛（花鸟），刘海粟（山水，人物），关山月（梅花），叶浅予（人物，舞者），石鲁（山水），张大千（山水、花鸟和人物）等。

In the period of Qin and Han Dynasties, the paintings on silk and the mural frescoes were brilliant and appealing.

In the period of Wei, Jin and Southern and Northern Dynasties, the mural frescoes had the very high artistic appreciation value.

The famous painters were as follows:Gu Kaizhi, Cao Buxing, Dai Kui, Lu Tanwei and Wei Xie.

From Sui and Tang Dynasties to Song Dynasty, the mural frescoes of Tang Dynasty dominated. *The Going Sightseeing in Spring* of Zhan Ziqian of Sui Dynasty is the earliest existing landscape painting. *The Riverside Scene on the Pure Brightness Festival* by Zhang Zeduan of Song Dynasty is a social genre painting.

The famous painters of this period were Zhan Ziqian, Yan Liben, Yuchi Yiseng, Wu Daozi, Li Sixun, Wang Wei, Zhang Xuan, Zhou Fang, Zhang Zeduan, Dong Yuan, Fan Kuan, Liu Songnian , Ma Yuan and Zhao Chang and so on.

In the period of Yuan Dynasty, the achievement of landscape painting and flower-bird painting was outstanding. The four big painters were Huang Gongwang, Wang Meng, Ni Zan and Wu Zhen.

In Ming Dynasty, there appeared Zhe School Painter Dai Jin, Su Zhou Wu School of Painting Shen Zhou, Wen Zhengming, Tang Yin and Qiu Ying, the School of Freehand Flower-Bird Painting (the freehand brushwork in traditional Chinese flower-bird painting) Xu Wei; and the School of Meticulous Flower-Bird Painting (the flower-bird fine brushwork) Bian Jingzhao and Lv Ji.

In Qing Dynasty, the four big monk painters were Hong Ren, Kun Can, Shi Tao and Zhu Da. The Eight Eccentric Artists in Yangzhou were Zheng Banqiao, Luo Pin, Huang Shen, Li Fangying, Gao Xiang, Jin Nong, Li Shan, and Wang Shishen. The Shanghai School of Painting were Ren Bonian and Wu Changshuo.

The famous painters in modern China are Qi Baishi (shrimp), Xu Beihong (horse), Pan Tianshou (eagle, hawk), Huang Binhong (landscape), Li Kuchan (flower and bird), Li Keran (landscape), Wang Xuetao (flower and bird), Liu Haisu (landscape and figure), Guan Shanyue (wintersweet, plum blossom), Ye Qianyu (figure, dancer), Shi Lu (lardscape), Zhang Daqian (landscape, flower, bird and figure).

第二节　中国的音乐·舞蹈

一、音乐

中国的传统乐器有：二胡、笛子、琴、筝、笙、箫、琵琶、锣、鼓。

中国古典音乐有十大名曲：《高山流水》《广陵散》《平沙落雁》《梅花三弄》《十面埋伏》《夕阳箫鼓》《渔樵问答》《胡笳十八拍》《汉宫秋月》和《阳春白雪》。

（一）《高山流水》

《列子·汤问》记载：伯牙善弹琴，钟子期善听琴。一次，伯牙弹了一首高山屹立、气势雄伟的乐曲，钟子期赞赏地说："巍巍乎志在高山。"伯牙又弹了一首惊涛骇浪、汹涌澎湃的曲子，钟子期又说："洋洋乎志在流水。"钟子期能深刻地领会伯牙所弹奏乐曲《高山流水》的内涵。从此，他们两人结成了知音，被传为千古佳话。

据文献记载，《高山流水》原为一曲。自唐代以后，《高山》与《流水》

Section 2　Chinese Music and Dance

一、Music

The traditional Chinese musical instruments are as follows: two-stringed bowed instrument with a lower register than Jinghu, flute, seven-stringed plucked instrument in some ways similar to the zither, 21or 25-stringed plucked instrument in some ways similar to the zither, reed pipe wind instrument, vertical bamboo flute, four-stringed plucked instrument with a fretted fingerboard; gong, and drum.

Ten most famous musical compositions of the classical Chinese music are as follows: *Lofty Mountain and Flowing Water, Guang Ling Verse, Wild Geese Alighting on the Sandbank, Three Stanzas of Plum-blossoms, Ambush on All Sides, Flute And Drum At Sunset, Dialogue Between Fisherman And Woodcutter, Eighteen Songs by Nomad Flute, Autumn Moon Over Han Palace*, and *Sunny Spring and White Snow*.

（一）*Lofty Mountain and Flowing Water*

According to the record of *Lieh-tzu · Tang Wen*, Bo Ya was good at playing the zither, to which Zhong Ziqi was good at listening. At one time, Bo Ya played a piece of music of erect mountain and majestic momentum, and Zhong Ziqi said with admiration that the towering appearance aimed at the high mountain. Bo Ya played another piece of music with the surge of the horrendous billows and terrifying waves. Zhong Ziqi said once more that it was multitudinous and aimed at the flowing water. Zhong Ziqi could deeply understand the connotation of the compositions—*Lofty Mountain and the Flowing Water* played by Bo Ya. Therefrom, they both became the bosom friends, and their story has been handed down through the ages.

According to the record of literature, *Lofty Mountain and Flowing Water* was

分为两首独立的琴曲。其中《流水》一曲，在近代得到更多的发展，曲谱初见于明代《神奇秘谱》（朱权成书于 1425 年）。管平湖先生演奏的《流水》曾被录入美国太空探测器的金唱片，于 1977 年 8 月 22 日发射到太空，向茫茫宇宙寻找新的"知音"。

（二）《广陵散》

《广陵散》又名《广陵止息》，是我国古代的一首大型器乐作品。据《神奇秘谱》载录，此曲原是东汉末年流行于广陵地区（即今安徽省寿县境内）的民间乐曲，曾用琴、筝、笙、筑等乐器演奏，现仅存古琴曲。

此曲之所以能跻身于十大古曲之一，还得部分归功于嵇康。魏末著名琴家嵇康因反对司马昭的专政而惨遭杀害。在临刑前，嵇康从容地弹奏此曲以为寄托。弹奏完毕，他叹息道：《广陵散》今天成为绝响。之后《广陵散》名声大振。人们在理解这首乐曲时又多了一层意义，它蕴涵了一种蔑视权贵、愤恨不平的情绪。

（三）《平沙落雁》

《平沙落雁》是一首展景抒怀的琴曲，又名《雁落平沙》《平沙》，作者传有唐代的陈子昂、宋代的毛逊、明代的朱权等，众说不一。该曲谱最早载于 1634 年（明末崇祯七年）刊印的藩王朱常涝纂集的《古音正宗》。此曲原为四段，在流传的过程中发展成六段、七段、八段等不一。

originally a piece of composition. After the Tang Dynasty, the composition was divided into two pieces of independent compositions of violin, one of which, the *Flowing Water* got more development in early modern times, and its music score was originally seen in the *Miraculous Secret Tablature* of Ming Dynasty (Zhu Quan wrote the book in 1425). The *Flowing Water* played by Mr. Guan Pinghu was once recorded into the golden record of the American space probe, which was launched into the space on August 22th, 1977, looking for a new bosom friend to the vast universe.

(二) *Guang Ling Verse*

Guang Ling Verse is also named *Guang Ling Cease*, and it was a piece of large instrumental music work in ancient China. According to the record of the *Miraculous Secret Tablature*, this piece of music was originally the folk music popular in the Guang Ling Region (present-day Shou County, An Hui Province) in the last years of the Eastern Han Dynasty, and it was once played with the instruments such as lyre, zither with 21or 25 string, reed pipe wind instrument, ancient 13-stringed instrument and so on. And now it is only preserved (conserved) in the ancient lyre music.

The reason why this music can rank among the top ten classical compositions was still partly because of Ji Kang. Ji Kang, the famous musician of the Late Wei Dynasty, who was good at playing the ancient Chinese Zither, was cruelly killed because he was opposed to the dictatorship of Sima Zhao. Before execution Ji Kang played this music calmly to repose his feeling in it. After he finished it, he sighed out that the *Guang Ling Verse* had become an inimitable music that day. Hereafter, the *Guang Liang Verse* rose to fame. When people understand this music, they add another layer of meaning that it contains a kind of feeling of despising bigwigs and resenting injustice.

(三) *Wild Geese Alighting on the Sandbank*

The Wild Geese Alighting on the Sandbank is a piece of music of showing scenery and expressing feeling played by ancient Chinese Zither, and it is also named *Flat Sandbank*. About the author, people have different opinions. According to legends, the author was Chen Zi'ang of Tang Dynasty, or Mao Xun of Song Dynasty,

《平沙落雁》是一首旋律优美流畅的七弦琴音乐。它的旋律描绘了大雁在遥远的地平线上盘旋，然后落在沙滩上的情景。

全曲以水墨画般的笔触，淡远而苍劲地勾勒出大自然寥廓壮丽的秋江景色，表现了清浅的沙流、万里的云程、天际群雁飞鸣起落的声情。曲意爽朗，乐思开阔，给人以肃穆而又富于生机之感。它借鸿雁之高飞远翔来抒发和寄托人们的胸臆，体现了古代人民对祖国美丽风光的热爱与赞美。

（四）《梅花三弄》

古琴曲《梅花三弄》又名《梅花引》《梅花曲》《玉妃引》，是中国古典乐曲中表现梅花的佳作，唐朝初年就在民间广为流传。全曲表现了梅花洁白芳香、凌霜傲雪的高贵品性，是一首充满中国古代士大夫情趣的琴曲。《枯木禅琴谱》说："曲音清幽，音节舒畅，一种孤高现于指下；似有寒香沁入肺腑，须从容联络，方得其旨。"

or Zhu Quan of Ming Dynasty and so on. The music score was first recorded in the book *Orthodox School of Ancient Music* compiled by the Seignior Zhu Changfang and printed (transcribed) in the year of 1634 (the seventh year of the Emperor Chongzhen, in late Ming Dynasty). This music had originally four paragraphs, and it has developed during the process of spreading into six paragraphs, seven paragraphs, and eight paragraphs and so on.

Wild Geese Alighting on the Sandbank is a piece of lyre music with smooth and melodious tunes. Its melody depicts the scene of wild geese's hovering on the distant horizon before alighting on the sandbank.

The whole music uses the brushwork like ink and wash painting to sketch elegantly and forcefully out the vast and magnificent scenery of the Autumn river in the nature, presenting the clear and shallow running sand, thousands of miles of clouds, the sound and emotion of groups of wild geese when they fly, sing, rise and fall up and down on the horizon. The meaning of the music is bright and clear, and the thinking of the music is very wide. It gives people the sense that is solemn and full of vitality. It uses swan geese's flying high and far to express and repose human feelings, embodying ancient people's love and praise of the beautiful scenery of the motherland.

（四）*Three Stanzas of Plum-blossoms*

The ancient Chinese Zither music *Three Stanzas of Plum-blossoms* is also named *Plum Blossom Melody*, *Plum Blossom Cantus*, and *Imperial Concubine Jade Melody*, and it is a masterpiece among the Chinese classical music to display plum blossoms. And it had already circulated widely in early Tang Dynasty. The whole music shows plum blossom's noble characters of being white and fragrant and rising higher than frost and defying snow, and it is a Zither music full of the temperament and interest of ancient Chinese intelligentsia. The book *Dead Wood Zen Music Scores* says: "The tones are clear and quiet, and the syllables of the tones are happy (entirely free from worry). A kind of loneliness and loftiness is expressed under the fingers, as if a kind of cold fragrance seeps into your inner heart. You must take it easy to connect every part , and then you can understand its purport. "

（五）《十面埋伏》

《十面埋伏》是一首著名的大型琵琶曲，堪称"曲中经典"。乐曲内容的壮丽辉煌、风格的雄伟奇特，在中国古典音乐中是罕见的。此曲最早见于 1818 年出版的华秋萍版《琵琶谱》，1895 年出版的李芳园编订的《南北派十三套大曲琵琶新谱》中将它改名为《淮阴平楚》。

乐曲是根据公元前 202 年楚、汉两军在垓下（今安徽省灵璧县东南）进行决战时，汉军设下十面埋伏的阵法，从而彻底击败楚军，迫使项羽自刎乌江这一历史事实加以集中概括谱写而成。"垓下决战"是中国历史上一次有名的战役。琵琶曲《十面埋伏》出色地运用音乐手段表现了这场古代战争的激烈战况，向世人展现了一幅生动感人的古战场画面。

（六）《夕阳箫鼓》

这是一首抒情写意的文曲，旋律优美流畅，在演奏中运用了各种琵琶演奏技法。此曲流传甚广，是琵琶古曲中的代表作品之一。乐谱最早见于 1875 年的抄本。1925 年前后，上海大同乐社根据此曲改编成丝竹乐曲《春江花月夜》。它犹如一幅长卷画面，把丰姿多彩的景色联合在一起，通过动与静、远与近、情与景的结合，使整个乐曲富有层次，高潮突出。音乐所表达的诗情画意引人入胜。

（五）*Ambush on All Sides*

It is a famous large lute music, and can be called as the classic of music. The splendid and spectacular music content with significant and peculiar music style is rare in the classical music. This music was first found in the book *Tablature of Lute* by Hua Qiuping published in the year of 1818, and it was renamed as *Huai Yin Ping Chu* by the book *New Music Scores of Chinese Lute of the Thirteen Big Compositions of the Southern and Northern Genres* compiled by Li Fangyuan and published in the year of 1895.

The music was based on the historical fact: In the year of 202 B.C. the two armies of Chu and Han fought a decisive battle at the place called Gaixia (present-day southeast of Lingbi County, Anhui Province). The Han troops designed the tactical deployment of the ten-sided ambush, beat the Chu troops thoroughly, and forced Xiang Yu to suicide beside Wu River. This music was composed to concentrately generalize the historical fact. The Decisive Battle at Gaixia was a famous battle in the history of China. The lute music *Ten-sided Ambush* uses the musical means excellently to show the fierce battle situation of the ancient war, and shows people a vivid and touching picture of the ancient battle field.

（六）*Flute And Drum at Sunset*

This is a piece of lyric and enjoyable literary music, and its melody is beautiful and mellifluous, and a variety of Chinese lute techniques are used when it is played. This music is spread widely, which is one of the representative works of the ancient music played by Chinese lute. Its music score was first found in the manuscript of 1875. Around the year of 1925, the Shanghai Great Unity Music Club adapted this music into the composition played by the traditional stringed and woodwind instruments, named as A *Night of Flowers and Moonlight by the Spring River*. It is like a picture of long scroll to link the rich and polychrome scenes together, and it makes the whole music full of gradations and highlights the climax through the combination of dynamic and static, farness and nearness, sentiment and scene. The poetic illusion expressed by the music is fascinating .

（七）《渔樵问答》

《渔樵问答》是一首流传了几百年的古琴名曲，反映的是一种隐逸之士对渔樵生活的向往，并希望摆脱俗尘凡事的羁绊。音乐生动形象，通过渔樵在青山绿水间自得其乐的情趣，表达出对追逐名利者的鄙弃。

乐曲采用渔民和樵夫对话的方式，题材集中精练，以上升的曲调表示问句，以下降的曲调表示答句，曲调飘逸潇洒，描绘出渔樵在青山绿水中悠然自得的神态。乐曲中时而出现伐木或摇橹的声响，使人形象地联想起渔樵生活的情景。

（八）《胡笳十八拍》

古琴曲《胡笳十八拍》是根据汉代以来流传的同名叙事诗而创作的琴曲，是中国音乐史上一首杰出的古典名曲。原诗作者一说为蔡琰，但《后汉书·蔡琰传》中未见记载，故难以定论。其音乐为唐人传谱。

乐曲分两大层次：前十来拍主要倾诉作者身在胡地时对故乡的思恋，后一层次则抒发出作者惜别稚子的隐痛与悲怨。乐曲以十分感人的乐调诉说了蔡琰一生的悲惨遭遇，反映了战乱给人民带来的深重灾难，抒写了主人公对祖国、对故土的深切思念，以及骨肉离别的痛苦感情。它曾被郭沫若称为"是一首自屈原《离骚》以来最值得欣赏的长篇抒情诗"。

（七）*Dialogue Between Fisherman and Woodcutter*

It is a famous piece of music played by Chinese ancient zither, which has been spread for hundreds of years. And what it reflects is a kind of yearning of hermits (recluses) for the life of fishermen and woodcutters, and the hope to get rid of the fetters of the secular world and worldly things. The music is vivid and visual, and it expresses through the temperament and interest of finding joy in their own way of the fishermen and woodcutters among the blue hills and green streams the disdain for the people to chase fame and wealth.

The music adopted the method of dialogue between the fisherman and woodcutter, whose subject is concentrated and refined. It indicates the interrogative sentences with the rising tune, and denotes the responses (answers) with the falling tune. Its tune (melody) is elegant, natural and unrestrained, and it describes the carefree and content mien of the fisherman and woodcutter in green mountains and rivers. The logging or sculling sound appears in the music from time to time, which makes people conjure up vividly the life scene of the fisherman and woodcutter.

（八）*Eighteen Songs by Nomad Flute*

The ancient Chinese music *Eighteen Songs by Nomad Flute* is a piece of Chinese Zither music, composed according to the spread narrative poem of the same name since the Han Dynasty, and it has been a outstanding piece of famous classical music in the musical history of China. A kind of parlance says that the composer of the original poem was Cai Wenji, but the record hasn't been found in the book of *Later Han Dynasty · the Biography of Cai Yan*, so it is difficult to make a conclusion. Its music is the tablature (music score) handed down by the people in Tang Dynasty.

The music is divided into two big levels — the first ten songs mainly pour out the longing (yearning) for hometown of the composer who was in the place of Hu (the Northern barbarian tribes in ancient China), and the latter part expresses the dull pain and sorrow and bitterness of the composer who was reluctant to part with her young kids. The music tells the miserable experience of Cai Yan's lifetime with a very touching tune, reflects the severe disasters brought to people by the chaos caused by war, and describes the protagonist's deep yearning for her motherland and

（九）《汉宫秋月》

在中国传统音乐中，同名异曲、异曲同名的现象很多，乐曲各个版本的历史渊源与流变往往需要艰苦的考证。比如，《汉宫秋月》就有琵琶曲、二胡曲、古筝曲、江南丝竹等不同版本。

此曲由一种乐器曲谱演变成不同谱本，且运用各自的艺术手段进行再创造，以塑造不同的音乐形象，这是民间器乐在流传中常见的情况。乐曲表现了古代宫女哀怨悲愁的情绪，以及一种无可奈何、寂寥清冷的生命意境。

（十）《阳春白雪》

现存琴谱中的《阳春》和《白雪》是两首器乐曲，相传这是春秋时期晋国的师旷或齐国的刘涓子所作，乐曲产生的年代没有确切的史料可以说明。唐朝显庆二年（657 年）吕才曾依琴中旧曲配以歌词。《神奇秘谱》在解题中说："《阳春》取万物知春，和风骀荡之意；《白雪》取凛然清洁，雪竹琳琅之音。"后来泛指高深的、不通俗的文学艺术。

hometown and the painful emotions of separation of the same flesh and blood. It was once praised by Guo Moruo as the long lyric poem that was the most worthy of appreciation since the *Lisao (Sorrow After Departure)* of Qu Yuan.

（九）*Autumn Moon over Han Palace*

Among traditional Chinese music, there is a lot of phenomenon of the same name with the different music or different music with the same name, and the historical origin and evolvement of music in different editions often require laborious (arduous) criticism. For example, the music *Autumn Moon Over Han Palace* has different editions such as Chinese lute music, Erhu music, Chinese zither music, South Yangzi string and pipe ensemble and so on.

This music has evolved into the different editions from a kind of music score by a kind of instrument, and they have used their own art means to re-create so as to mould the different musical images, which is the situation commonly seen during the spread of the folk instrumental music. This music expresses the plaintive (piteous) and heavy-hearted sentiment of the ancient maid in the imperial palace and a kind of life artistic conception of having no other alternative and being lonesome and chill.

（十）*Sunny Spring and White Snow*

The Sunny Spring and the *White Snow* in the existing tablature (music score) are two pieces of instrumental music. According to the legend, they were composed by Shi Kuang of Jin State or Liu Juanzi of Qi State in the Spring and Autumn Period, and there hasn't been exact historical data that can manifest the time when the music appeared. In the second year of Xian Qing, Tang Dynasty (in the year of 657), Lv Cai matched it with lyric in accordance with the old music. The book the *Miraculous and Secret Tablature* said in the explanation of the title, "*The Sunny Spring* takes the meaning that all things know that the spring has been coming and the gentle breeze is oscillating lightly. And the *White Snow* takes the sounds of the awe-inspiring and clean snow, bamboo, gem and jade." Later, it refers to the profound and unpopular literature and art in general.

二、舞蹈

中国的舞蹈艺术有着悠久的历史和很高的成就，包括古典舞蹈、民族舞蹈和当代歌舞。

(一) 古典舞蹈

中国古典舞蹈艺术的最高成就是唐代舞蹈。唐代舞蹈中，最有代表性的是礼仪乐舞《十部乐》和唐代大曲《霓裳羽衣舞》。

《十部乐》

《十部乐》包括《燕乐》《清乐》《西凉乐》《天竺乐》《高丽乐》《龟兹乐》《安国乐》《疏勒乐》《康国乐》《高昌乐》。它以隋朝的《七部乐》和《九部乐》为基础，集中了魏晋南北朝以来各个民族及域外的乐舞，并加以规范化。《十部乐》的表演主要用于外交、庆典和宴会等场合，场面宏大，气氛庄严，具有强烈的多民族色彩和鲜明的礼仪性，代表了唐代礼仪乐舞的最高水平。

《霓裳羽衣舞》

《霓裳羽衣舞》是唐代大曲的代表作，曲调由唐明皇创作，独舞由杨贵妃表演。舞蹈采用了传统的优美舞法，同时，融合了西域舞蹈中精彩的旋转技巧，配以美妙的音乐，逼真地再现了缥缈的仙境，塑造了美丽的仙女形象，取得了很高的艺术成就，从而成为中国舞蹈艺术史上的杰作。

(二) 民族舞蹈

中国民族舞蹈艺术中，最具有代表性的是新疆维吾尔族的舞蹈和云南傣

二、Dance

Chinese dance art has a long history and high achievments, including the classical dance, the ethnic dance, the contemporary singing and dancing.

（一）Classical Dances

The highest achievment of the Chinese classical dance art was the Tang Dynasty dance. Among the Tang Dynasty dances, the most representatives were the ritual dance *Ten Kinds of Music* and the Tang Dynasty large-scale music *raiment of Rainbows and Feathers Dance.*

Ten Kinds of Music

Ten Kinds of Music included *Yan Music, Qing music, Xiliang Music, Tianzhu Music, Gaoli Music, Qiuci Music, Anguo Music, Shule music, Kangguo Muisc* and *Gaochang Music.* They were based on the Sui Dynasty's *Seven Kinds of Music* and *Nine Kinds of Music*, integrating the music and dances of different ethnic groups and regions since the Wei, Jin, Southern and Northern Dynasties and standardizing them. The performance of *Ten Kinds of Music* was mainly used on such occasions as diplomacy, ceremonies, banquets and so on, with grand scenes, solemn atmosphere, strong multi-ethnic color and distinct etiquette, representing the highest level of the ritual dance in the Tang Dynasty.

Raiment of Rainbows and Feathers Dance

Raiment of Rainbows and Feathers Dance was the representative of the large-scale music of Tang Dyansty, whose melody was composed by the Emperor Xuanzong of Tang, with a solo dance performed by the Magnificent Concubine. The dance adopted the graceful traditional dance methods, at the same time, integrated the wonderful rotating skills in the western region dances with the wonderful music, vividly reproducing an ethereal fairyland, shaping a beautiful fairy image, and achieving very high artistic achievments, thus becoming a masterpiece in the history of Chinese dance art.

（二）Ethnic Dances

Among the Chinese ethnic dances, the most representatives are the Dance of

族的孔雀舞。

新疆维吾尔族的舞蹈

中国的维吾尔族自古居住在中国的西北部，有着历史悠久的文化艺术传统。维吾尔族舞蹈继承了古代鄂尔浑河流域和天山回鹘族的乐舞传统，又吸收了古代西域乐舞的精华，经过长期的发展和演变，形成了具有多种形式和特殊风格的舞蹈艺术，并广泛流传在新疆维吾尔自治区各地。

云南傣族的孔雀舞

孔雀舞是云南傣族传统的表演性舞蹈，中国当代著名舞蹈艺术家杨丽萍以其孔雀舞闻名全国。虽然孔雀舞没有音乐旋律的伴奏，伴奏乐器仅有脚鼓、锣、钹等打击乐器，但并不显得单调。孔雀舞风格轻盈灵秀，情感表达细腻，舞姿婀娜优美，是傣族人民智慧的结晶，具有很高的审美价值。

（三）当代歌舞——《小苹果》

现在，在中国大陆，有一支比较流行的歌舞，就是筷子兄弟创作的《小苹果》。

筷子兄弟是由导演、演员肖央和音乐人、演员王太利组成的，集"编剧、导演、演员、音乐创作、歌手"于一身的极具创新力量和艺术才华的复合型组合。2007 年 5 月底，他们携音乐电影大作《男艺妓回忆录》登陆互联网，引起爆炸式传播。其作品朴素幽默、细节突出、深刻感人，横扫了当年互联网视频短片领域的各项大奖。2010 年，他们推出"11 度青春系列电影"之《老男孩》，吸引了众多眼球，点击量过亿，被观众评为"祭奠逝去的青春时代的最强音"，开启了全新的"微电影"行业。筷子兄弟也成了"怀旧、青春、梦想"的代言人，获得了"60 后"到"90 后"几代人的喜爱与尊重。

Xinjiang Uygur and the Peacock Dance of Dai Ethnic Group in Yunnan Province.

Dance of Xinjiang Uygur

The Uygur people of China have lived in the northwest of China since ancient times, with a long history of cultural and artistic traditions. The Uygur dance has inherited the music and dance traditions of the ancient Orkhon River Basin and the Huihu people of Tianshan Mountain, and absorbed the essence of the music and dance of ancient western region. After a long period of development and evolution, it has formed the dance art with a variety of forms and a special style , widespread in various parts of Xinjiang Uygur Autonomous Region.

Peacock Dance of Dai Ethnic Group in Yunnan Province

The Peacock Dance is a traditional performance dance of Dai Ethnic Group in Yunnan Province. Yang Liping, a famous contemporary Chinese dance artist, is famous all over the country for her Peacock Dance. Although the Peacock Dance is not accompanied by musical melody, only such percussion instruments as foot drum, gong, cymbal and so on, it doesn't seem monotonous. The Peacock Dance is lightsome in style, delicate in emotional expression and graceful in posture, which is the crystallization of the Dai people's wisdom with the high aesthetic value.

（三）Contemporary Singing and Dancing —*Little Apple*

Now, in the Mainland of China, there has been a more popular singing and dancing *Little Apple* created by the chopstick brothers.

The chopstick brothers are the combination of the compound type with the highly innovative power and the artistic talent. They integrate the scriptwriter, the director, the performer, the music producer and the singer, and they are made up of the director and actor Xiao Yang, and the musician and actor Wang Taili. At the end of May, 2007, they brought the music movie masterpiece *Memoirs of the Male Geisha* to come on the stage of the internet and caused the explosive spread. Their work was simple and humorous, its details were outstanding, profound and touching, and it scooped all kinds of big awards in the field of the internet video clips. In 2010, they released the *Old Boy*, one of the *Eleven Degrees Youth Film Series*, and it

筷子兄弟的寓意或许是指这两个兄弟之间的关系是密切合作、不可分割的，就像一双筷子一样不可分割。只有当它们团结一致、互相协调、密切配合的时候，它们才能够发挥夹东西的作用；否则，当仅有一只筷子的时候，是不能用来夹东西的。同样，只有当他们两个兄弟团结一心、密切合作的时候，他们才能够创作出优秀的音乐作品和电影作品。

第三节　中国的戏剧·电影

一、戏剧

中国各地的传统戏曲有 300 多种，主要有北京的京剧、山东的吕剧、河北梆子、浙江的越剧、河北的评剧、安徽的黄梅戏、湖南的花鼓戏等。

（一）山东的吕剧

山东的简称是鲁，可是，山东的戏剧，为什么叫吕剧，而不叫鲁剧呢？原因有以下几种。

1. 自 1911 年春节，民间艺人孙中心在刘官村用纸糊的毛驴演唱了《王小赶脚》，人们便把它称为"驴戏"。由于这个称号欠雅，经一些文人的推敲，音译成了"吕戏"。1915 年前后，原属博兴县七区的谭家村（今已划为

attracted a lot of eyeballs. Its click volume was more than one hundred million. It was appraised as the strongest voice by the audience to honor the lost youth, and opened up the brand-new micro film industry. The chopstick brothers also became the spokespersons of nostalgia, youth and dream, and they have obtained the love and respect of a few generations from the late sixties to the late nineties.

I guess that the meaning of the chopstick brothers is that the relationship between the two brothers is closely cooperative and inseparable, just like a pair of chopsticks. Only when they work hand in glove, coordinate with each other, and unite as one, can they perform the role of clipping. Otherwise, a piece of chopstick cannot be used to clip food. For the same reason, only when the brothers coordinate closely and unite wholeheartedly, can they create fine musical works or movies.

Section 3 Chinese Dramas and Movies

一、Dramas

There are more than three hundred kinds of traditional operas around China. There are mainly the Beijing Opera, the Lv Opera of Shandong, the Wooden Clapper of Hebei Province, the Yue Opera of Zhejiang Province, the Ping Opera of Hebei Province, the Huangmei Opera of Anhui Province, the Flower Drum Opera of Hunan Province and so on.

(一) Lv Opera of Shandong

Shandong is called Lu for short, but why is the opera of Shandong called as Lv Opera, not Lu Opera? There are several reasons as follows.

1. Since the Spring Festival of 1911, after the folk artisan Sun Zhongxin performed the opera *Wang Xiao (a porter) Serves With a Donkey for Transportation* with the paper donkey in the village Liu Officer, people called the opera as the

广饶县）老艺人时殿元也曾以纸糊毛驴化装演唱过《王小赶脚》，受到了群众的欢迎。1923年，这种"驴戏"进了济南府，演出的主要剧目是《吕洞宾打药》。当地群众不明白这个剧种的来源，只听说叫"驴戏"，又由于主要剧目是"吕"字打头，所以观众就把它称为"吕戏"。

2. 据博兴的老艺人回忆说，吕剧的"吕"字，原是二十五户为一闾的"闾"字，"闾戏"的意思是街坊邻里戏、家乡戏。以后在辗转、流传中，把"闾"简化为"吕"。也有人说，过去说琴书，大多是两口子或一家人搭档，演唱的内容又多系反映男女爱情的；两口为"吕"，因而就叫"吕戏"。

3. 吕戏原来称为"捋戏"，此说有二。一种说法是：由于演唱时主要伴奏乐器是坠琴，按奏坠琴的手指是上下捋动，故名为捋戏；又因我国音乐十二律中的阴律有六种，总称"六吕"，因而将"捋戏"改称为"吕戏"。另一种传说是：当年为这种戏起名时，有的老艺人说，这种戏演唱时顺藤摸瓜，捋着蔓子捋到底，就叫它"捋戏"吧。又因为捋与吕同音，遂定名为"吕戏"，现在称之为"吕剧"。

Donkey Opera. Because the title was not elegant enough, it was transliterated into the Lv Opera by some deliberation of some literati . Around the year of 1915, the old entertainer Shi Dianyuan who belonged originally to the Pond Home Village of Seven District, Boxing County (now it has been zoned as Guangrao County), also once used the paper donkey to perform in disguise the opera *Wang Xiao Serves With a Donkey for Transportation*, and was welcomed by the masses. In the year of 1923, this kind of donkey opera entered the provincial capital Jinan, and the main play that was performed was *Lv Dongbin Buys Medicine*. The local people didn't know the source of the opera, and only heard that it was called as the donkey opera, still because the name of the main play began with the character Lv, the spectators called it as the Lv Opera.

2. According to the recall of the old entertainer of Boxing, the character "Lv" of the Lv Opera, was originally the character "闾（neighbourhood）" which meant a village of twenty-five families. The meaning of the 闾 opera referred to the neighbour play or the hometown play. Later, the character "闾" was simplified as the character "吕" during its circulating around. But some people still said that in the past when the pianology was performed, it was mostly a couple or a family as partners, and the content of the performance was mostly to reflect the love between the male and the female. Two "mouths" constitute the character "吕", therefore it was called Lv Opera.

3. The "吕" Opera was originally called as the "捋"（Stroke）Opera. There are two sayings about it. The first saying is as follows: Because the main accompaniment instrument was the pendant lyre when the opera was performed, and the performer's fingers stroked up and down when they were playing the pendant lyre, it was named as the "捋"（Stroke）Opera. In addition, because there were six kinds of negative laws of the twelve laws of our country's music, and they were called as the six "Lv" in general, people renamed the Stroke Opera the Lv Opera. The other legend is as follows: In the year when the kind of opera was named, some old entertainers said that, when the kind of opera was performed, the performers would follow the vine to get the melon, and stroke the vine to the bottom, then they called it the Stroke

（二）北京的京剧

在中国的传统戏曲中，京剧是最有代表性的。实际上，京剧原来也是一种地方戏，它 18 世纪末形成于清代的京城——北京，所以叫作京剧。它在全国的影响最大。

京剧角色：京剧有着细致的角色分工。女角统称为"旦"，男角统称为"生"。旦角儿，又分为"青衣""花旦""老旦""武旦"等。"生角儿"又细分为"小生""老生"和"武生"等。滑稽的人物，脸上画一块儿白色图案，称为"小丑"。正直豪爽或者凶猛奸诈的人物，脸上画的是彩色图案，称为"净"，俗称花脸。

京剧服装：大致采用的是明代服装的样式，颜色大红大绿，黄白黑蓝，色泽鲜明，对比强烈。

中国京剧有"四大名旦"：梅兰芳、程砚秋、荀慧生、尚小云。

其他的著名京剧演员：周信芳、马连良、谭鑫培、盖叫天。

梅兰芳的代表剧作有《贵妃醉酒》《霸王别姬》。

《贵妃醉酒》：主要描写杨玉环醉后自赏怀春的心态。杨玉环是唐朝皇帝唐玄宗李隆基的妃子。有一天，贵妃杨玉环奉唐明皇之命在百花亭侍宴，届时明皇驾转西宫梅妃处，贵妃失宠苦闷，借酒浇愁，酒醉回宫。

Opera. Because the character "㧪 (stroke)" had the same pronunciation as the character "吕", the kind of opera was named the "吕" (Lv) Opera.

(二) Peking Opera of Beijing

The Peking Opera is the most representative one among the traditional Chinese operas. In fact, the Peking Opera is also a kind of local opera, which formed in the capital of the Qing Dynasty — Peking, in the late 18th century, therefore, it was called Peking Opera. Its influence is the biggest in the whole country.

The roles of the Peking Opera: It has the detailed role assignment. The female roles are collectively referred to as "Dan"; and the male roles are collectively referred to as "Sheng". The female character types are additionally divided into "the Black Cloth" "the Multicoloured Female" "the Old Female" "the Valorous Female" and so on. The male character types are detailedly divided into "the Young Man" "the Old Man" "the Valorous Man", and so on. The funny character, on whose face a piece of white pattern is painted, is called the Clown. The righteous and great-hearted character or the fierce and fraudulent (treacherous) character, whose face the multicolored pattern is painted on, is called "the Clean", commonly known as the multicoloured face or the painted face.

The costume of the Peking Opera uses generally the style of the Ming Dynasty clothing, and its colour is gaudy and showy, including black, white, yellow, and blue. And it is bright in color, and has the intense color contrast.

The top four female roles of the Chinese Peking Opera were Mei Lanfang, Cheng Yanqiu, Xun Huisheng and Shang Xiaoyun.

The other famous Peking Opera actors: Zhou Xinfang, Ma Lianliang, Tan Xinpei and Gai Jiaotian.

Mei Lanfang's representative plays are the *Drunken Concubine* and *Farewell to My Concubine*.

The *Drunken Concubine* describes mainly Yang Yuhuan's mindset of self-admiration and becoming sexually awakened (being in love) after she was drunken. Yang Yuhuan (Yang Jade Bracelet) was the concubine of Li Longji, Tang Minghuang, the Emperor of Tang Dynasty. One day, the noble concubine Yang

《霸王别姬》：公元前 204 年，西楚霸王项羽与汉军作战，战败回营，汉军围困数重。到了晚上，闻汉军四面大营皆有楚歌声，项羽大惊。满怀愁绪之下，他在帐中饮酒。项羽有位很宠爱的妃子，叫虞姬。当晚，虞姬凄然自刎，项羽也流下热泪，左右都不敢抬头看他，这就是历史上的"霸王别姬"。

二、电影

中国电影起源于 19 世纪末 20 世纪初的上海。1896 年 8 月 11 日，上海徐园内的"又一村"放映"西洋影戏"，这是中国第一次放映电影。1905 年，北京丰泰照相馆的创办人任庆泰拍摄了由谭鑫培主演的京剧《定军山》片段，这是中国人自己摄制的第一部影片。1977 年电影生产开始复苏。1980—1984 年，年平均产量达 120 部左右，每年观众观影人次平均在 250 亿左右，中国电影进入一个蓬勃发展的新时期。2012 年，中国电影年产量高达 745 部。2013 年，全年总票房达到 217.69 亿元人民币，全国共有银幕 18195 块。2015 年，全年总票房达到 440.69 亿元人民币，全国共有银幕 31626 块。

中国电影行业的发展历程与中国电影导演的发展嬗变密切相关，从某个角度看，可以说，中国电影导演的发展嬗变也正反映了整个中国电影行业的

Yuhuan was ordered by the Emperor Tang Minghuang to serve him with dinner at the Hundred-flower Pavilion. At the appointed time, the Ming Emperor turned to the western palace, the place of concubine Mei. The noble concubine Yang Yuhuan was out of favour and anguished. And then she drowned her sorrows in wine, and went back to her palace after she was drunken.

Farewell to My Concubine: In the year 204 B.C., the overlord of the Western Chu Xiang Yu combated with the Han army, and returned to the camp after being defeated, and then the Han army besieged them circle upon circle. In the evening, Xiang Yu heard that the songs of Chu were all around the camp of the Han army, and was frightened full of melancholy, drinking in the tent. Xiang Yu had a favorite concubine, named Consort Yu. On the night, Consort Yu cut her throat mournfully, Xiang Yu also wept over with hot tears, and all the entourages didn't dare to look up at him. This was just the Overlord Bade Farewell to His Concubine in the history.

二、Movies

Chinese movies originated in the late 19th and early 20th centuries. On August 11th, 1896, the Western Leather-Silhouette Show was projected in Another Village in Xu Yuan, Shanghai, which was the first film screening in China. In 1905, Ren Qingtai, the founder of the Beijing Fengtai Photo Studio shot a segment of the Peking Opera *Ding Jun Shan* starring Tan Xinpei, which was the first film made by Chinese people themselves. In 1977, the film production began to revive. From 1980 to 1984, the average annual output was about 120 movies; the average annual audience were about 25 billion; and China movies had entered a new period of vigorous development. In the year of 2012, the output of Chinese movies was up to 745. In 2013, the total box office income for the whole year was 21.769 billion yuan of RMB, and there were 18195 screens altogether in China. In the year of 2015, the total box office income for the whole year was 44.069 billion yuan of Renminbi, and the whole country had 31626 screens altogether.

The development process of Chinese film industry has been closely related to the evolution of Chinese film directors. From a certain perspective, it can be said that

发展历程。大陆电影学院派把中国的电影导演大体上划分为六代。

第一代电影导演：即默片时期的电影导演，大致活跃于 20 世纪初叶到 20 世纪 20 年代末。代表人物有：郑正秋、张石川、但杜宇、任彭年、沈浮、史东山、邵醉翁、何非光及杨小仲等。作为中国电影的奠基者，第一代导演从中国传统的叙事艺术和舞台戏曲中吸收了很多手法，密切联系时代的要求，重视电影的社会教化作用。早期电影在内容上难免浅陋芜杂，在艺术上也较幼稚，具有试验性特征，但其拓荒作用功不可没。

第二代导演：主要活跃在 20 世纪 30 年代和 40 年代，是中国电影第一个"黄金时代"的创造者。代表人物有：费穆、蔡楚生、孙瑜、袁牧之、郑君里、吴永刚、程步高、沈西苓、史东山、桑弧及汤晓丹等。这一时期，中国电影就思想内容而言，开始真正从单纯的娱乐中解放出来，比较深入地反映社会生活；在艺术上，这一代导演最大的特点是写实主义，同时，他们注意把"写实"和电影化结合起来；在故事情节上，他们强烈地追求戏剧悬念、戏剧冲突和戏剧程式。

第三代导演：中华人民共和国成立之后走上影坛的导演艺术家。代表人物有：谢晋、谢铁骊、凌子风、崔嵬、成荫、水华、郭维、鲁韧和王炎等。他们遵循现实主义原则表现生活的本质，深入展现矛盾冲突，并在民族风格、地方特色、艺术意蕴等方面，都进行了十分有益的探索。

the evolution of Chinese film directors has also reflected the development process of the entire Chinese film industry. The film academicism in the mainland has generally divided the Chinese film directors into six generations.

The first generation of film directors were the film directors during the period of the silent movies, who were active roughly from the early 20th century to the late 1920s. The representatives were Zheng Zhengqiu, Zhang Shichuan, Dan Duyu, Ren Pengnian, Shen Fu, Shi Dongshan, Shao Zuiweng, He Feiguang and Yang Xiaozhong, etc. As the founders of the Chinese movies, the first generation of directors absorbed a lot of skills from the traditional Chinese narrative arts and the stage dramas, kept in close touch with the demands of times, and attached great importance to the social enlightenment. The early films were unavoidably crude in contents and naive in arts, with some experimental characteristics, but its pioneering role was indispensable.

The second generation of film directors were active mainly in the 1930s and 1940s, and they were the creators of the first golden age of Chinese movies. The representatives included Fei Mu, Cai Chusheng, Sun Yu, Yuan Muzhi, Zheng Junli, Wu Yonggang, Cheng Bugao, Shen Xiling, Shi Dongshan, Sang hu, Tang Xiaodan and so on. During this period, the Chinese films, in terms of ideological contents, began to be truly liberated from the pure entertainment and began to reflect the social life in depth. In arts, the greatest characteristic of this generation of directors was realism, and at the same time, they paid attention to the combination of realism and filmmaking. In the story plots, they strongly pursued the dramatic suspense, dramatic conflicts and dramatic programs.

The third generation of directors were the directing artists who walked onto the moviedom after the founding of the People's Republic of China. The representatives were as follows: Xie Jin, Xie Tieli, Ling Zifeng, Cui Wei, Cheng Yin, Shui Hua, Guo Wei, Lu Ren, Wang Yan and so on. They followed the realistic principle to express the essence of life, deeply showing the contradictions and conflicts, and carried on a very beneficial exploration in the national style, local characteristic and artistic

第四代导演：20 世纪 60 年代北京电影学院的毕业生。代表人物有：谢飞、吴贻弓、吴天明、黄蜀芹、滕文骥、丁荫楠、郑洞天、颜学恕、张暖忻和胡柄榴等。他们提出中国电影应该"丢掉戏剧的拐杖"这一理念，打破戏剧式结构，提倡纪实性，追求质朴自然的风格和开放式结构，注重主题与人物的意义，并从生活中的凡人小事中去开掘社会与人生的哲理。

第五代导演：20 世纪 80 年代从北京电影学院毕业的一批导演，是中国电影发展历程中最辉煌的一代。代表人物有：张艺谋、陈凯歌、田壮壮、霍建起、顾长卫、吴子牛、黄建新、李少红和冯小宁等。他们作品的特点是主观性、象征性、寓意性十分强烈。在选材、叙事、塑造人物、镜头语言、画面处理等方面，他们既遵从传统，又有所创新。

第六代导演：20 世纪 80 年代中后期进入北京电影学院、20 世纪 90 年代后开始执导电影的一批年轻导演。代表人物有：贾樟柯、王全安、姜文、王小帅、张元、娄烨、陆川和张杨等。他们注重以电影为媒介来考察当代都市普通人的生活状态，新一代青年在历史转型时期的迷茫、困惑和无所适从在他们的镜头下被真实地记录下来。

中国大陆著名的电影导演张艺谋和著名女演员巩俐曾经是一对恋人，而且密切合作。张艺谋与巩俐合作的电影有《红高粱》《菊豆》等。

implication and so forth.

The fourth generation of directors were the graduates from the Beijing Film Academy in 1960s. The representatives were Xie Fei, Wu Yigong, Wu Tianming, Huang Shuqin, Teng Wenji, Ding Yinnan, Zheng Dongtian, Yan Xueshu, Zhang Nuanxin, Hu Bingliu and so forth. They put forward the idea that the Chinese films should throw away the dramas as crutches, break the dramatic structure, advocate the features of documentary, pursue the plain and natural style and open structure, pay attention to the meaning of themes and characters, and explore the philosophy of society and life from the trivial things in life.

The fifth generation of directors were the graduates from the Beijing Film Academy in 1980s, and they have formed the most brilliant generation in the developmental process of the Chinese films. The representatives are Zhang Yimou, Chen Kaige, Tian Zhuangzhuang, Huo Jianqi, Gu Changwei, Wu Ziniu, Huang Jianxin, Li Shaohong, Feng Xiaoning and so on. Their works are characterized by strong subjectivity, symbolism and allegorization. They not only follow the traditions but also make innovations in the selection of materials, narration, character shaping, lens language, picture processing and other aspects.

The sixth generation of directors are the young directors who entered the Beijing Film Academy in the mid or late 1980s and began to direct films in 1990s. The representatives are Jia Zhangke, Wang Quan'an, Jiang Wen, Wang Xiaoshuai, Zhang Yuan, Lou Ye, Lu Chuan, Zhang Yang and so on. They pay attention to the film as a medium to investigate the living conditions of contemporary urban ordinary people. And the confusion, bewilderment and cluelessness of the new generation of young people in the period of the historical transformation are truly recorded under their cameras.

Zhang Yimou, One of the most famous director in the mainland of china and Gong Li, one of the most famous actress were once a couple of lovers, who were once hand in glove with each other. The movies on which Zhang Yimou and Gong Li cooperated closely with each other include *Red Sorghum, Ju Dou* and so on.

（一）《红高粱》

该片改编自莫言的同名中篇小说，以童稚的视野回忆了"我爷爷余占鳌（姜文饰）"和"我奶奶（巩俐饰）"的故事。"我奶奶"19岁时心不甘情不愿地出嫁，在路上与轿夫余占鳌生出感情。走到十八里坡时，两个人都没能按捺住心中的欲火，于高粱地里野合。"我奶奶"怀上余占鳌的骨肉嫁给了李大头。李大头死后，"我奶奶"撑起李家的烧酒作坊。不久，余占鳌正式成为"我爷爷"，并独创酿制好酒十八红的方法。抗日战争期间，"我爷爷"和"我奶奶"在"我爹"九岁时连手谱写了一曲悲歌。

（二）《菊豆》

这是一部由导演张艺谋执导，演员巩俐、李保田主演的剧情电影，于1990年上映。影片讲述的是20世纪中叶一个江南农村的故事。染坊老板杨金山为了传宗接代，续弦娶了年轻姑娘菊豆为妻。杨金山上了年纪又身患暗疾，没有生育能力。日子一长，菊豆偷偷与他的养子杨天青产生了爱情并生下一子天白。四岁时，天白无意将瘫了下肢的杨金山撞入染池淹死。由于吃人的"礼教"，菊豆与杨天青依然过着表面婶侄关系的生活。最终，渐已成人的天白怒杀与母"通奸"的生父杨天青。菊豆万念俱灰，纵火烧掉了杨家世代相传的祖业"杨家染坊"。这部影片荣获第九届中国香港电影金像奖"十大华语片之一"和法国第四十三届戛纳国际电影节"首届路易斯·布努埃尔特别奖"。

（一）*Red Sorghum*

This movie was adapted from the medium-length novel with the same name of Mo Yan, and it recalls in a childish perspective about the story of his grandfather Yu Zhan'ao (acted by Jiang Wen) and his grandmother (acted by Gong Li). His grandma got married reluctantly when she was 19 years old, and on the road she produced emotion toward the bearer of the sedan chair — Yu Zhan'ao . When they got to the Eighteen Mile Slope, they could not restrain the fire of the desire in their hearts and had the illicit sexual relations in the red sorghum field. His grandma conceived a child of Yu Zhan'ao and married Li Big Head. After Li Big Head died, his grandma supported the liquor-making workshop of the family Li. Soon, Yu Zhan'ao became his grandpa formally, and he originated the method of brewing the good wine: Eighteen Red. During the Anti-Japanese War, his grandpa and grandma composed a song of elegy together when his dad was 9 years old.

（二）*Ju Dou*

It is a feature film directed by the director Zhang Yimou and acted by the performers Gong Li and Li Baotian, which was released in the year of 1990. What the film narrates is as follows: In the middle of the 20th century, in a village south of the Yangtze River, the dyehouse owner Yang Jinshan remarried the young girl Ju Dou in order to have a son to continue his family line. Yang Jinshan got on in years and suffered from the unmentionable disease, infertility. As time went on, Ju Dou secretly fell in love with his adopted son Yang Tianqing, and gave birth to a son named Tian Bai. When he was 4 years old, Tian Bai bumped unwittingly Yang Jinshan whose lower limbs were paralyzed into the dye pool, and Yang Jinshan was drowned. Because of the life-destroying feudal ethics and rites, Ju Dou and Yang Tianqing still lived the life of the ostensible aunt-nephew relationship. In the end, Tian Bai who had gradually been adult killed angrily his biological father Yang Tianqing who had sexual relationship with his mother. Ju Dou was blasted, and set on a fire to burn up the ancestral property of family Yang — the Dyehouse of Family Yang, which was passed down from generation to generation. The film won the 9th China Hong Kong Film Golden Image Award—One of the Top 10 Chinese Films, and the Special Award

三、电视剧

自从 1958 年 6 月我国第一部电视剧与观众见面以来，中国国产电视剧已经走过了风风雨雨的 60 多年。60 多年来，中国电视剧从无到有，从蹒跚学步到快速发展。现在，电视剧已经成为覆盖最广、受众最多、影响最大的文化形态，成为文化领域中最具活力的中坚产业，成为中国向世界传播中国声音、展现中国风貌、阐发中国精神的重要载体。

纵观中国电视剧的发展历程，可以分为六个阶段。

第一阶段：20 世纪六七十年代是电视剧的起步时期。

1958 年 6 月 15 日，北京电视台播出了家庭伦理剧《一口菜饼子》，此剧成为中国第一部电视剧。虽然这部电视剧全长只有 20 分钟，但标志着我国电视剧发展的初步探索。这一时期的电视剧作品基本没有太大的娱乐性，只有较强的宣传作用。1961 年的《桃园女儿嫁窝谷》、1962 年的《绿林行》、1966 年的《焦裕禄》等电视剧皆以正面典型人物作为作品主体。1978 年 5 月，由许欢子、蔡晓晴导演的电视剧《三亲家》播出，这是新时期录制的第一部彩色电视剧，也是电视单本剧时代的开始，它成为中国电视剧复苏史上的标志性作品。

第二阶段：20 世纪 80 年代是电视剧的发展阶段。

20 世纪 80 年代，观看电视成为人们颇为普遍的精神消费。1981 年，王扶林导演完成了中国大陆第一部长篇电视剧《敌营十八年》，这是中国大陆

of the First Luis Bunuel at the Forty-third Cannes International Film Festival in France.

三、Teleplays

Since the first television play met with the audience in China in June, 1958, the Chinese domestic teleplays have already passed 60 years of ups and downs. Over the past 60 years, the Chinese teleplays have passed from nonexistence into existence, and from a toddler to rapid development. At present, the teleplay has become the cultural form that has covered the widest area, with the most audience and the biggest influence, and has become the backbone industry with the most dynamic in the cultural field and the important carrier for China to disseminate Chinese voices, to show Chinese styles and features and to expound Chinese spirits.

The developmental process of the Chinese teleplay can be divided into the following six stages.

The first stage was the 1960s and 1970s — the start-up stage.

On the 15th of June,1958, the Beijing Televison Station broadcast the family ethnics drama, *A Mouthful of Vegetable Cake*, which became the first teleplay of China. Although the full length of the teleplay was only 20 minutes, it marked the initial exploration of the developmental process of Chinese teleplay. The teleplays of this period were basically not very entertaining, only with the stronger propaganda function. *The Daughter of the Peach Orchard Married to Wogu* of 1961, *The Greenwood Trip* of 1962, the *Jiao Yulu* of 1966 and other dramas all took positive and active characters as the main body of works. In May, 1978, the television drama *Three Families of Relatives* directed by Xu Huanzi and Cai Xiaoqing was broadcast, which was the first color television drama recorded in the new era, also the beginning of TV single play, and it has become an iconic work in the resuscitating history of Chinese television dramas.

The second stage was the 1980s, the developmental stage.

In the 1980s, watching TV had become a more common spiritual consumption for Chinese people. During this period, in 1981, the director Wang Fulin completed

的第一部电视连续剧。1983 年，《霍元甲》作为大陆引进的第一部香港电视剧，播出时盛况空前。1985 年，一部描写旧上海的电视剧《上海滩》震惊了所有的上海人。同年，北京电视艺术中心拍摄的电视连续剧《四世同堂》播出，因其深刻的思想性和高度的文学性引起了强烈反响，成为当时社会舆论的中心话题。1986 年，中国第一部采用特技拍摄的电视连续剧《西游记》播出，获得了极高评价。同年，上海电视台制作的电视连续剧《济公》应运而生，每晚家家窗户里传出的都是它的主题歌。1987 年春节，36 集大型古装电视连续剧《红楼梦》第一次以日播的形式在中央电视台播出，造就了中国电视剧史上"难以逾越的经典"。

第三阶段：20 世纪 90 年代—2000 年是电视剧的繁荣时代。

1990 年后，电视剧渐渐成为电视台工作的重心，电视剧内容逐步多样化，以满足不同观众的需求，古装剧、武侠剧、红色经典剧、公安题材剧、反腐题材剧、都市家庭剧、青春偶像剧陆续出现。1990 年出品的 50 集电视连续剧《渴望》作为中国第一部大型室内电视连续剧，在中央电视台播出，开创了真正意义上的中国长篇电视情节剧的历史。继电视连续剧《渴望》之后，20 世纪 90 年代，陆续出现了《爱你没商量》《皇城根儿》《京都纪事》《我爱我家》《东边日出西边雨》《英雄无悔》《儿女情长》等一系列经典剧目。值得一提的是，1990 年出品的古装神话历史剧《封神榜》，在服装、神怪造型上都开风气之先。 还有，1991 年上映的 25 集电视连续剧《编辑部的故事》，是我国第一部电视系列喜剧。1994 年，中国第一部情景喜剧《我爱我家》开播，因为这部剧导演英达也被称作"中国情景喜剧教父"。另外，历史题材的电视剧，包括《水浒传》《三国演义》《宰相刘罗锅》等都给观众留下了深刻印象。同时期，中国香港和台湾也输送了许多优秀的电视剧

the first full-length TV series of the mainland *In the Enemy Camp for* 18 *Years*, and this was the first television series in the mainland. In the year of 1983, *Huo Yuanjia*, as the first Hong Kong TV series introduced to the mainland was in unprecedented pomp and circumstance when it was broadcast. In 1985, a television drama *Shanghai Beach* about the old Shanghai shocked all the Shanghainese. In the same year, the TV series *Four Generations Under One Roof* by Beijing TV Art Center was broadcast, and because its profound thoughts and high degree of literature caused a strong response, it became the central topic of the public opinion at that time. In 1986, China's first television series filmed by stunts, *Journey to the West* was broadcast, and it has been highly praised. In the same year, the TV series *Buddha Jih* came into being, and its theme song came out of all the windows of every family in each night. In addition, in the Spring Festival of 1987, *A Dream of Red Mansions*, a large scale television series in ancient costume and with thirty-six episodes was broadcast on China Central Television Station in the form of daily broadcast for the first time, creating the insurmountable classic in the history of Chinese television dramas.

The third stage was from the 1990s to the year 2000, the prosperous times.

After the year of 1990, television dramas have gradually become the focus of TV stations' work, and the contents of TV dramas are gradually diversified to meet the needs of different audiences. Ancient costume dramas, knight-errant dramas, dramas of red classics, dramas of public security theme, dramas of anti-corruption subject, urban family dramas and youth idol dramas appeared consecutively. *Aspiration* produced in 1990 was a fifty-episode television series. As the first large-scale indoor television series in China, it was broadcast on China Central Television Station, which initiated the history of Chinese full-length television melodrama in a real sense. Following after *Aspiration*, in the 1990s, there appeared consecutively a series of classic dramas such as *I Love You Anyway, The Foot of the Imperial City, Kyoto Chronicle, I Love My Family, The Sun Rises in the East and the Rain Falls in the West, Hero Without Regrets*, and *Be Immersed in Love*, etc. It was worth mentioning that *The Legend of Deification*, a mythological historical drama in ancient

作品，例如《新白娘子传奇》《神雕侠侣》等。在即将跨越千禧之时，《还珠格格》轰动了亚洲，它风靡全球各国华人圈并打破了中国电视剧收视纪录。《还珠格格》（第一部）于 1998 年播出，《还珠格格》（第二部）于 1999 年播出，《还珠格格》（第三部）于 2003 年播出。

第四阶段：21 世纪初，电视剧形成多元并存的新格局。

这一时期，电视剧创作艺术日趋成熟，大众文化的趣味性和艺术作品的专业性开始相容，造就了中国电视剧多元创作的新格局。2002 年，一部《激情燃烧的岁月》引发了国人对峥嵘岁月的集体回忆。2005 年，《亮剑》引爆了一批军旅剧的热播。两年后，一部几乎没有任何知名演员主演的《士兵突击》，开创了一种全新的现实主义军旅剧审美。与此同时，曾经以"婆婆妈妈"为主的家庭伦理剧也愈来愈见"品质效应"，如《金婚》《媳妇的美好时代》等。自 2006 年起，《乡村爱情》系列剧，通过几对年轻人的爱情生活和创业故事，多角度地展现了一幅当代农村青年的爱情生活画卷。2007 年，《奋斗》火遍全国，剧中倔强骄傲、成熟独立的夏琳一角成为新一代女性的代表。此外，同年，中国电视剧获得了三个世界第一——生产数量世界第一、播出数量世界第一、观众数量世界第一。此后，2008 年的《闯关东》与 2009 年的《潜伏》都从不同题材中找到了独特的支点。

costume, produced in the year of 1990, led the fashion in both costume and genie modelling. In addition, *the Stories from the Editorial Board*, a 25-episode television series released in the year of 1991 was the first television comedy series in China. In 1994, China's first sitcom, *I Love My Family* was broadcast, and because of this comedy, the director Ying Da has also been known as the godfather of the Chinese sitcom. Besides the above dramas, the historical television dramas including *Outlaws of the Marsh, Romance of the Three Kingdoms*, and *The Prime Minister Liu Luoguo* and the like left a deep impression on the audience. At the same period, China Hong Kong and Taiwan also supplied many excellent teleplay works such as *New Legend of Madame White Snake*, and *The Return of the Condor Heroes* and all that. When we were about to cross the millennium, *Princess Pearl* caused a sensation in Asia, and swept about the Chinese circles of every country all over the world and broke the viewing record of Chinese television dramas. *Princess Pearl I* was released in 1998; *Princess Pearl II* was broadcast in 1999; *Princess Pearl III* was presented in 2003.

The fourth stage was at the beginning of the 21st century, and a new pattern of multiple coexistence took shape.

During this period, the art of television drama became increasingly mature, and the interest of popular culture and the professionalism of artistic works began to be compatible, which created a new pattern of diversified creation of Chinese television dramas. In the year of 2002, *The Years of Passion Burning* triggered the country's collective memories of eventful years. In 2005, *Drawing Sword* made a batch of military dramas a massive hit. Two years later, *Soldiers Sortie* starred by almost no well-known actors pioneered a completely new kind of realistic military drama aesthetics. At the same time, the family ethics dramas which used to focus on the household affairs were increasingly showing the quality effect, such as *Golden Wedding* and *Wonderful Times of Wives* and so forth. Since the year of 2006, the drama series *Country Love*, through the love life and business stories of several pairs of young people, presented from multiple perspectives a picture scroll of love life of contemporary rural youth. In the year of 2007, *Striving* went viral around the country, and Xia Lin, a role in the play who was stubborn, proud, mature and independent

第五阶段：网络时代，网剧兴起。

2014 年，各大视频网站纷纷打出"网络自制剧元年"的称号。2015 年网剧蓬勃发展，为电视剧的题材和表达方式都增加了多样性。2015 年度"十大受欢迎网剧"几乎都是根据网络小说改编而来。例如，《甄嬛传》《芈月传》《琅琊榜》《锦绣未央》《遇见王沥川》《花千骨》《择天记》《三生三世十里桃花》《楚乔传》等。

第六阶段：当下，电视剧的内容更多地聚焦现实。

从 2010 年之后，中国国产电视剧就已经迎来了现实主义题材的小高峰。例如，有表现中国社会城乡改革大潮的《浮沉》《马向阳下乡记》《温州一家人》《平凡的世界》《温州两家人》等作品。2017 年，现实题材剧似乎迎来了春天，诸如《人民的名义》《鸡毛飞上天》《白鹿原》等，占据了 2017 年电视剧的半壁江山。此外，还有《我的前半生》《欢乐颂 2》《情满四合院》《生逢灿烂的日子》《猎场》《急诊科医生》等也都有很好的收视率。

其中，根据中国古典四大名著小说改编的电视连续剧《西游记》《红楼梦》《三国演义》和《水浒传》深受中国民众喜爱。

has become the representative of a new generation of women. In addition, in 2007, Chinese television dramas won the first place in three aspects in the world——the production quantity was number one; the broadcast quantity ranked the first; and the audience quantity took first place. Since then, both *Brave the Journey to Northeast* of 2008 and *Lurking* of 2009 found the unique supporting point from different themes.

The fifth stage was the era of internet, and the internet dramas have been springing up.

In the year of 2014, many major video websites presented one after another the title—the First Year of the Network Homemade Dramas. In 2015, the online dramas boomed, which added variety to the themes and expressions of television dramas. This year's top ten most popular online dramas, such as *Legend of Concubine Zhen Huan, Legend of Miyue, Nirvana in Fire, The Princess Wei Yang, Remembering Wang Lichuan, The Journey of Flower, Choose the Day to Remember, To the Sky Kingdom, Princess&Agents* and others were almost all adapted from online novels.

The sixth stage is at the present time, and the contents of television dramas focus more on reality.

Since 2010, the Chinese television dramas such as *Ups and Downs, Ma Xiangyang Goes to the Countryside, Legend of Entrepreneurship, The Ordinary World, The Two Wenzhou Families* and so forth, which represented the great tide of the urban and rural social reform in China, have ushered in a small peak of realistic theme. In 2017, the teleplays of the realistic theme seem to be welcoming the spring, and such teleplays as *In the Name of People, A Chicken Feather Flying to Heaven*, and *White Deer Plain* and the like took up half share of the teleplays this year. In addition, *The First Half of My Life, Ode to Joy II, Quadrangle Dwellings Are Full of Feelings, Living in Bright Days, Game of Hunting*, and *Emergency Medicine Specialists* and so on have also had a very nice audience rating.

The teleplay series including the *Journey to the West, The Dream of Red Mansions, The Romance of the Three Kingdoms* and *The Outlaws of the Marsh* are very popular with Chinese people. They were all adapted from the four great classical Chinese novels.

（一）《西游记》

《西游记》作者吴承恩，又名《西游释厄传》，成书于16世纪明朝中叶，主要描写了唐僧、孙悟空、猪八戒、沙悟净师徒四人去西天取经，历经九九八十一难的故事。

（二）《红楼梦》

《红楼梦》作者是清代作家曹雪芹。《红楼梦》以贾宝玉和林黛玉的爱情为线索，描写了大家族贾府由盛到衰的变迁故事。

（三）《三国演义》

《三国演义》由元末明初小说家罗贯中所著，是中国第一部长篇章回体历史演义小说，描写了从东汉末年到西晋初年之间近100年的历史风云。全书既反映了三国时代的政治和军事斗争，又反映了三国时代各类社会矛盾的渗透与转化，概括了这一时代的历史巨变，塑造了一批叱咤风云的英雄人物。

赤壁之战是《三国演义》中的精彩片段，是中国历史上著名的以弱胜强的战争之一。208年7月12日（汉献帝建安13年）曹操率领水陆大军，号称百万，发起荆州战役讨伐孙权。孙权和刘备组成联军，由周瑜指挥，在长江赤壁（今湖北省赤壁市西北，一说今嘉鱼县东北）一带大破曹军，从此奠定了三国鼎立的格局。赤壁之战是第一次在长江流域进行的大规模江河作战，也是孙、曹、刘各家都派出主力参加的唯一战事。

（一）*Journey to the West*

Journey to the West whose author is Wu Cheng'en, is also named *The Pilgrimage to the West to Dispel Adversities,* and was written in the middle period of Ming Dynasty in the 16th century. It mainly describes the story that the master Tang Monk and his three apprentices including Sun Wukong (Monkey King), Zhu Bajie (Pig Eight Warning), and Sha Wujing (Sand Awaken Clean) went to the west to fetch the Buddhist scriptures and go through nine times nine eighty-one adversities.

（二）*The Dream of Red Mansions*

A Dream of Red Mansions whose author is Cao Xueqin, the writer of Qing Dynasty, describes the vicissitude of the big family Jia using the love story between Jia Baoyu and Lin Daiyu as a clue.

（三）*The Romance of the Three Kingdoms*

The Romance of the Three Kingdoms was written by Luo Guanzhong, the novelist of the late Yuan Dynasty and the early Ming Dynasty. It was the first novel in China which was the full-length and historical romance novel with a caption for each chapter. It describes the drastic historical changes of nearly one hundred years from the late Eastern Han Dynasty to the early Western Jin Dynasty. The whole book reflects the political and military struggles, the infiltration and transformation of all kinds of social contradictions in the Three Kingdoms Period, outlines the enormous historic changes of this era, and shapes a batch of heroic figures riding the whirlwind.

The Battle of Red Cliff is a wonderful piece of *The Romance of the Three Kingdoms,* one of the famous fights of defeating a strong and superior force with a weak and backward force in the history of China. On July 12th, 208 A.D., (the 13th year of Jian An of Emperor Xian of Han Dynasty) Cao Cao led the amphibious main forces, being known as one million, to launch the battle of Jingzhou, and then sent a punitive expedition against Sun Quan. Sun Quan and Liu Bei constituted the allied forces, commanded by Zhou Yu, and destroyed Cao's army in the area of Red Cliff of the Yangtze River (Today it is in the northwest of the city Red Cliff, Hu Bei Province. The other saying says that it is in the northeast of present-day Jia

（四）《水浒传》

《水浒传》又名《忠义水浒传》，简称《水浒》，创作于元末明初。作品由施耐庵所著，罗贯中编校。《水浒传》是汉语文学中最具史诗特征的作品之一，也是中国历史上最早用白话文写成的章回体小说之一。全书描写北宋末年以宋江为首的108位好汉在梁山泊起义，以及聚义之后接受招安、四处征战的故事。作品版本众多，流传极广，脍炙人口，对中国乃至东亚的叙事文学创作都有着极其深远的影响。（"水浒"的"浒"即水边，"水浒"也是指水边，泛指水边发生的种种故事。）

第四节　中国的曲艺·杂技

一、曲艺

曲艺是中国民间艺术形式，是中国说唱艺术的总称，可以划分为四大类：相声、鼓曲、快板、评书。

Yu County), and since then the pattern of the tripartite confrontation of the Three Kingdoms was laid. The Battle of Red Cliff was the first large-scale riverine fight held in the Yangtze River Basin, also the only fight which all the three emperors of Sun, Liu and Cao sent their main forces to take part in.

（四）*The Outlaws of the Marsh*[*]

The Outlaws of the Marsh is also named *The Loyal and Righteous Outlaws of the Marsh*, with a shortened name *Water Margin*. It was written between the late Yuan Dynasty and the early Ming Dynasty, during the turning of Yuan and Ming Dynasties. The novel was written by Shi Nai'an, and edited by Luo Guanzhong. *The Outlaws of the Marsh* is one of the works that have the most characteristics of epic in Chinese literature, and one of the earliest written novels in vernacular with a caption for each chapter in Chinese history. The whole book describes the story that one hundred and eight brave men headed by Song Jiang uprose in the marsh of Liang Mountain, then accepted amnesty and went on campaigns everywhere after getting together and uprising. There are many versions of the work, which has spread extensively, and has won universal praise. It has had a far-reaching influence on the narrative literature of China and even East Asia.

Section 4   Chinese Qu Yi and Acrobatics

一、Qu Yi

Qu Yi is the Chinese folk art form, the generic term for the Chinese rap art, which can be divided into four types including Comic Talk, Drum Music, Clapper

---

* The meaning of the Chinese character "浒" is water side. "水浒" also means water side.
  "水浒传" refers to a variety of stories that occurred on the waterfront (in the marsh).

（一）相声

中国的相声有三种：单口相声、对口相声、群口相声。单口相声是一个人说，对口相声是两个人说，群口相声是三个以上的人说。其中，对口相声最为普遍。

相声的表演手段，以说为主，兼用学、逗、唱。"说"，是叙述故事，描绘人物；"学"是模仿各种动作和声音；"逗"是逗乐取笑；"唱"是学唱各种曲调。

当代中国著名的相声演员有侯宝林、郭启儒、郭全保、马三立、唐杰忠、姜昆、马季、冯巩、笑林、李金斗、石富宽和侯耀文等。

（二）鼓曲

鼓曲中最著名的是山东大鼓。山东大鼓是北方大鼓的"鼻祖"，相传形成于明朝末期，已有350多年的历史。20世纪后期以来，山东大鼓逐渐趋于衰落，现在仅有少数演员还能演出。

（三）快板

快板就是有节奏地打着竹板儿或者铜板讲故事。山东快书是最有影响的一种快板形式。山东快书是起源于山东省的汉族传统曲艺形式，已有100多年的历史。它最早流行于山东、华北、东北各地，中华人民共和国成立后发展到遍及全国。

（四）评书

评书就是讲故事。民间比较流行的评书故事是《杨家将》和《岳飞传》。

Talk and Story Telling.

（一）The Comic Talk

There are three kinds of Chinese Comic Talk including the Monologue Comic Talk, the Comic Cross Talk, and the Group Cross Talk. The Monologue Comic Talk is performed by one person, the Comic Cross Talk is performed by two persons and the Group Cross Talk is performed by more than two persons. Among them, the Comic Cross Talk is the most popular one.

The performance means of the Comic Talk give priority to speaking, and use concurrently the measures including learning, teasing and singing. "Speaking" is to narrate a story and describe figures; "learning" is to mimic all kinds of actions and sounds; "teasing" is to clown around and provoke laughter, and "singing" is to learn to sing all kinds of tunes.

The famous Cross Talk performers in contemporary China include Hou Baolin, Guo Qiru, Guo Quanbao, Ma Sanli, Tang Jiezhong, Jiang Kun, Ma Ji, Feng Gong, Xiao Lin, Li Jindou, Shi Fukuan and Hou Yaowen and so on.

（二）The Drum Music

Among the Drum Music, the most famous one is the Shandong Big Drum. The Shandong Big Drum is the ancestor of the northern big drum. According to legend, the Shandong Big Drum was formed in late Ming Dynasty, with a history of more than 350 years. Since the late 20th century, the Shandong Big Drum has tended to decline gradually, and now only a few actors can perform it.

（三）The Clapper Talk

The Clapper Talk is rhythmic storytelling accompanied by bamboo or copper clappers. The Shandong Clapper Ballad is the most influential form of the Clapper Talk. The Shandong Clapper Ballad is the traditional art form originated from the Han ethnic group in Shandong Province, with a history of more than 100 years. It was first popular in Shandong Province, North China and Northeast China, which developed and spread throughout all the country after the founding of PRC.

（四）The Story Telling

The Story Telling is exactly to tell stories. The most popular storytellings are *The*

《杨家将》是一部中国历史英雄传奇系列故事。

现存作品有两种，比较有影响的一种是《北宋志传》，后易名《杨家将演义》。它对北宋前期的一些人物和事件加以演义，讲述了杨家四代人——杨继业、杨延昭、杨宗保、杨文广戍守北疆、精忠报国的动人事迹。

《杨家将》《薛家将》《呼家将》构成了中国通俗小说史上著名的"三大家将小说"。

《岳飞传》主要讲述了岳飞从一个贫家子弟成长为一代抗金名将，最后含冤屈死的悲壮生平故事。岳飞（1103—1141 年），南宋著名军事家、民族英雄。

二、杂技

杂技就是"各种技艺"的意思，包括各种体能和技巧的表演艺术。现代杂技特指演员靠自己的身体技巧完成一系列高难度动作的表演性节目。

中国的杂技艺术历史悠久，源远流长，是中华民族珍贵的优秀文化遗产。中国的杂技之乡有很多，其中，历史最悠久、群众基础最深厚、在海内外影响最大的是河北省沧州市吴桥县。

中国杂技的传统项目有顶碗、转碟和走钢丝等。

Generals of the Yang Family (Yang Warriors) and *The Legend of Yue Fei*.

The Generals of the Yang Family is a series of stories of the legendary heroes in Chinese history.

About the stories, there are two kinds of existing works, and the more influential version was named the *Romance of the Northern Song Dynasty*. Later it was renamed *Legend of Warriors of Yang Family*, which developed some figures and events of the Early Northern Song Dynasty,and narrated the stirring stories of the four generations of the Yang Family — Yang Jiye, Yang Yanzhao, Yang Zongbao and Yang Wenguang who garrisoned the northern border area and repaid the country with the supreme loyalty.

The Generals of the Yang Family, The Generals of the Xue Family, and *The Generals of the Hu Family* constitute three famous great novels of Family Generals in the history of Chinese popular novels.

The Legend of Yue Fei mainly narrates the tragic life of Yue Fei from a child of a poor family to grow up to become a famous general against the Jin forces, who finally suffered wrongs and was persecuted to death. Yue Fei was born in 1103, while died in the year of 1141, who was the famous strategist and national hero of the Southern Song Dynasty.

二、Acrobatics

Acrobatics means all kinds of feats, including a variety of physical and technical performing arts. Modern acrobatics refers to the performance program in which the performers perform a series of difficult movements with their own physical skills.

China's acrobatic art can go back to ancient times with a long history, which is a precious cultural heritage of the Chinese nation. There are many famous acrobatic villages in China, among which Wuqiao County in Cangzhou City of Hebei Province has the longest history, with the deepest mass foundation and biggest influence at home and abroad.

Traditional programs of Chinese acrobatics include Balancing a Stack of Bowls on the Head, Plate Spinning and Tightrope Walking.

顶碗：演员头部顶一摞瓷碗，表演劈叉、倒立、金鸡独立等技巧动作，难度极大，常常震惊观众。

转碟：演员们用一根长约一米，粗如铅笔的竿子顶着碟底晃动旋转，碟子看上去像迎风而立的荷叶，又像飞舞的彩蝶。这个节目表演起来优美而抒情。

走钢丝：演员在拉紧、悬空的钢丝绳上行走、跳舞或表演翻筋斗。它以其悠久的历史、独特的风格、精湛的技艺和惊险的表演令人赞叹。

思考题：

谈谈你对中国传统的艺术形式的体验和认识。

When performing Balancing a Stack of Bowls on the Head, the performer with a stack of bowls on his or her head, performs the acrobatic acts such as splits, handstand, posing as a pheasant standing on one foot and so on, which often shock the audience with its extreme difficulties.

When Plate Spinning is performed, the performers use a pole that is about one meter long and as thick as a pencil to support the bottom of the plate, shaking and spinning, so that the plates look like lotus leaves standing against the wind, also butterflies flying in the air. The program is beautifully and lyrically performed.

When Tightrope Walking is performed, the performer walks, dances or somersaults on the tightening-hanging wire rope. It makes the audience amazing with its long history, unique style, superb skills and breathtaking performance.

Thinking Question:

Talk about your experience and understanding of traditional Chinese art forms.

第七章　中国的旅游

中国有着丰富的旅游资源和众多的风景名胜。

第一节　中国的旅游资源

世界上的旅游资源，可以分为两大类：一类是自然旅游资源，另一类是人文旅游资源。

中国的六大古都包括北京、西安、洛阳、开封、南京、杭州，都是著名的旅游城市。

中国有九大旅游区：中原旅游区、东部沿海旅游区、川汉旅游区、华南热带景观旅游区、西南岩溶地貌旅游区、西北"丝绸之路"旅游区、东北旅游区、北疆塞外旅游区、青藏高原游牧区。

第一，中原旅游区，位于黄河中下游地区，包括陕西，山西、河南、河北、山东、北京市和天津市，简称华北地区，也称中央旅游区。其名胜主要有：北京、西安、洛阳、开封、承德、曲阜、济南、青岛、秦皇岛、太原、大同、泰山、华山、五台山。

Chapter 7   Chinese Tourism

China has rich tourism resources and many scenic spots.

Section 1   Chinese Tourism Resources

The tourism resources in the world can be divided into two categories: one is the natural tourism resources, and the other is the humanistic and cultural resources.

The top six ancient capitals of China include Beijing, Xi'an, Luoyang, Kaifeng, Nanjing and Hangzhou, which are all famous tourist cities.

China's top nine tourist areas are as follows: the Central Plains Tourist Area, the Eastern Coastal Tourist Area, the Chuan-Han Tourist Area, the South China Tropical Landscape Area, the Southwest Karst Landform Tourist Area, the Northwest Tourist Area on the Silk Road, the Northeast Tourist Area, the Northern Border Tourist Area Beyond the Great Wall , and the Qinghai-Tibetan Platean Nomadic Area.

Firstly, The Central Plains Tourist Area is situated in the middle and lower reaches of the Yellow River, including Shaanxi, Shanxi, Henan, Hebei, Shandong, Beijing and Tianjin, which is called for short the North China, and also called as the Central Tourist Area. Its scenic spots mainly have Beijing, Xi'an, Luoyang, Kaifeng, Chengde, Qufu, Jinan, Qingdao, Qinhuangdao, Taiyuan, Datong, Tai Mountain, Hua

第二，东部沿海旅游区。这一旅游区位于长江下游和黄海、东海之滨，包括浙江、江苏、安徽、江西四省和上海市，简称华东地区。主要名胜有：中国最大的海港和工商业城市上海、南京、杭州、苏州、无锡、扬州、绍兴、富春江、新安江水力发电站、钱塘江观潮、佛教圣地普陀山、雁荡山、黄山、九华山、庐山。

第三，川汉旅游区。即长江上游、中游地区，包括湖北省、湖南省、重庆市和四川省中、东部地区。主要名胜有：长江三峡、成都、重庆、乐山大佛、峨眉山、武当山、神农架、川西自然保护区、武汉、黄鹤楼、赤壁、荆州古城、衡山游览区、长沙、岳麓书院（中国古代著名"四大书院"之一）、毛泽东故乡韶山冲、洞庭湖、岳阳楼、张家界森林公园。

第四，华南热带景观游览区。包括广东省、福建省、海南省、台湾省，地处南部沿海，接近香港和澳门地区以及东南亚，属于亚热带。主要观光地有：广州、福州、厦门、武夷山、丹霞山、海南岛、深圳、珠海、汕头、厦门经济特区。

第五，西南岩溶地貌旅游区。包括广西、云南、贵州三个省、区。这是中国岩溶地貌的主要分布区。主要观光地有：西双版纳风光、桂林山水、贵州黄果树瀑布、昆明古城、滇池、西山游览区、石林风景。

Mountain and Wutai Mountain.

Secondly, the East Coastal Tourist Area is situated in the lower reaches of the Yangtze River and the shores of the Yellow Sea and the East Sea, including Zhejiang, Jiangsu, Anhui, Jiangxi four provinces and Shanghai city, which is called for short the East China. The main scenic spots include China's largest seaport and the industrial and commercial city Shanghai, Nanjing, Hangzhou, Suzhou, Wuxi, Yangzhou, Shaoxing, the Fuchun River, the Xin'an River Hydropower Station, the Qiantang River Bore, the Buddhist holy land Putuo Mountain, the Yandang Mountain, the Yellow Mountain, the Jiuhua Mountain and the Lu Mountain.

Thirdly, the Chuan-Han Tourist Area, namely it is the upper and middle reaches of the Yangtze River, including Hubei Province, Hunan Province, Chongqing City and the middle and eastern regions of Sichuan Province. The main scenic spots include the Three Gorges of Yangtze River, Chengdu, Chongqing, the Giant Buddha at Leshan Mountain, the Mount Emei, the Wudang Mountain, the Shennongjia Forestry District, the Western Sichuan Nature Reserve, Wuhan, the Yellow Crane Tower, the Red Cliff, the Jingzhou Ancient City, the Hengshan Mountain Tourist Area, Changsha, the Yuelu Academy (one of the famous top four academies in ancient China), Mao Zedong's hometown Shaoshan Chong, Dongting Lake, Yueyang Tower and Zhangjiajie National Forest Park.

Fourthly, the South China Tropical Landscape Tourist Area includes Guangdong Province, Fujian Province, Hainan Province and Taiwan Province, which is situated in the south coastal region, close to Hong Kong, Macao and the Southeast Asia, belonging to the subtropics. The main tourist sites include Guangzhou, Fuzhou, Xiamen, Wuyi Mountain, Danxia Mountain, Hainan Island, Shenzhen, Zhuhai, Shantou and Xiamen Special Economic Zone.

Fifthly, the Southwest Karst Landform Tourist Area includes Guangxi, Yunnan and Guizhou three provinces and region. This is the main distribution area of the Chinese karst landform. The main tourist sites include the Xishuangbanna Scenery, the Guilin Landscape, the Yellow Fruit Tree Waterfall in Guizhou, the Kunming

第六，西北"丝绸之路"旅游区。所谓的"丝绸之路"，是指中国古代与阿拉伯和欧洲进行丝绸贸易的一条陆上通道。全长7000多公里。"丝绸之路"在中国境内经过陕西、甘肃和新疆三个省及自治区。"丝绸之路"上的游览地有：敦煌石窟、敦煌壁画、麦积山石窟雕塑、嘉峪关、玉门关、楼兰遗址、戈壁滩大沙漠、刘家峡水库、吐鲁番盆地、火焰山、兰州、酒泉、乌鲁木齐、喀什。

第七，东北旅游区。这一旅游区包括东北三省：辽宁、吉林、黑龙江。游览区有：五大连池（火山湖）、镜泊湖（火山堰塞湖）、哈尔滨冰灯、沈阳古城、鞍山千山、大连避暑胜地、吉林滑雪、长春八大部（净月潭）。

"八大部"是伪满洲国的八大统治机构，即治安部（军事部）、司法部、经济部、交通部、兴农部、文教部、外交部、民生部的统称。这些政治机构与伪国务院、综合法衙（司法检察机关）都建在长春新民大街附近，形成以地质宫为中心的建筑群。

第八，北疆塞外旅游区。即位于长城以北的内蒙古自治区，有辽阔的草原风光，独特的蒙古风情。

Ancient Town, the Dianchi Lake, the West Mountain Tourist Region and the Stone Forest Scenic Spot.

Sixthly, it is the Northwest Tourist Area on the Silk Road. The so-called Silk Road refers to the overland route on which the ancient China traded in silk with Arabian Peninsula and Europe, and its total length was more than 7,000 kilometers. The Silk Road passed through three provinces including Shaanxi, Gansu and Xinjiang within the territory of China. The tourist sites on the Silk Road include the Dunhuang Grottoes, the Dunhuang Frescoes (Murals), the Maijishan Grotto Statues, the Jiayu Pass, the Jade Gate Pass, the Loulan Ruins, the Gobi Desert, the Liujiaxia Reservoir, the Turpan Depression, the Flaming Mountain (the Volcano land), Lanzhou, Jiuquan, Urumchi, and Kashi.

Seventhly, it is the Northeast Tourist Area. This tourist area includes three northeast provinces including Liaoning, Jilin and Heilongjiang. There are the tourist regions such as the Five Connective Lakes (volcanic lake), the Jingbo Lake (volcano dammed lake), the Harbin Ice Lantern, the Shenyang Ancient Town, the Anshan Thousand Mountain, the Dalian Summer Resort, the Jilin Skiing, and the Changchun Eight Main Departments (the Pure Moon Pool).

The Eight Big Departments were the eight big governing bodies of the pseudo Manchuria State, namely the umbrella name of the eight ministries including the Ministry of Public Security (the Military Department), the Ministry of Justice, the Economy Ministry, the Ministry of Communications, the Ministry of Developing Agriculture, the Department of Culture and Education, the Ministry of Foreign Affairs, and the Ministry of the People's Livelihood. These political institutions and the pseudo State Council and the Synthetical Government Offices (the judicial and procuratorial organs) were all built near the New-human Street in the city of Changchun and formed the architectural complex centered on the Geological Palace.

Eighthly, the Northern Border Tourist Area beyond the Great Wall is located in the Inner Mongolia Autonomous Region on the north, and it has the vast grassland scenery and unique Mongolian custom.

第九，青藏高原游牧区。包括西藏、青海两个省、区和四川西部，是世界上最高的地区。主要的景点有：世界最高峰珠穆朗玛峰、古老而美丽的高原城市拉萨、独特的高原寺庙布达拉宫和大昭寺。

第二节　中国名城选介

北京和西安这两座城市是中国古都的代表，也是中国最大的旅游城市。

一、北京

北京至今已有三千多年的历史。早在公元前 1057 年，这里就是诸侯国燕国的都城，当时称作"蓟"。

938 年，契丹人在北方建立了辽国，这里成为辽国的陪都，改称"南京"，又叫"燕京"。

1153 年，女真族建立的金朝迁都于此，称其为"中都"。

1260 年，成吉思汗的孙子忽必烈到达中都，7 年后即 1267 年，把中都定为元朝首都，并以大宁宫为中心建立了"大都城"。

1403 年，明成祖朱棣在此建都，改称"北京"，并重新修建了北京城。

Ninthly, the Qinghai-Tibetan Plateau Nomadic Area includes Qinghai Province and the Tibet Autonomous Region and the western part of Sichuan Province, and it is the highest area in the world. The main scenic resorts include the world's highest peak the Mount Everest, the ancient and beautiful plateau city Lhasa, and the unique plateau temple — the Potala Palace and the Jokhang Temple.

Section 2 Selective Introduction of the Famous Chinese Cities

The two cities — Beijing and Xi'an are the representatives of the ancient capitals of China, which are also the biggest tourist cities.

一、Beijing

Beijing has hitherto had a history of more than three thousand years. As early as in the year of 1057 before Christ, here was exactly the capital of the vassal state Yan, and it was called "Ji" at that time. (Ji means thistle, a kind of plant.)

In the year of 938, the Khitan people established the Liao State in the north, and here became the second capital of the Liao State. Then it was renamed as Nanjing, also called "Yanjing".

In the year of 1153, the Gold Dynasty that was established by the Jurchen ethnic group moved its capital here, and called it as Chung Tu (the Mid Capital).

In the year of 1260, Genghis Khan's grandson Kublai Khan arrived in the Mid Capital. Seven years later, in the year of 1267, he set the Mid Capital as the capital of the Yuan Dynasty, and built the Big Capital City centered on the Daning Palace.

In the year of 1403, the Ming Emperor Zhudi established its capital here, and changed its name into "Beijing", and reconstructed the city of Beijing.

北京最著名的地方就是天安门广场。天安门是首都北京的象征。天安门城楼庄严美丽，广场的西侧是人民大会堂，东侧是中国国家博物馆，南侧是毛主席纪念堂，广场中央矗立着人民英雄纪念碑，附近的中南海是中共中央和国务院的所在地。所以说，天安门广场是中国首都的政治中心。

北京最主要的街道是长安街。长安街西起复兴门，东至建国门，全长六公里，宽度为六七十米。

北京最著名的名胜古迹就是长城和故宫。万里长城坐落在北京城西北 70 多公里的八达岭上，全长 6700 多公里，横跨中国北部六个省、市。长城在战国时期开始修建。今天的长城大多是明代重新修建的，被称作是"世界建筑史上的奇迹"。

故宫是中国现存最大、最完整的帝王宫殿和古代建筑群，位于北京城中心，始建于 1406 年，用了 14 年的时间才建成，里面住过明、清两代 24 位皇帝。

颐和园，位于北京城的西北郊，是一座秀丽的皇家园林，是现存的中国古代最大的皇家园林。

圆明园，原来是中国最大的皇家园林，曾被称作"万园之园"。可惜的是，这座世界名园，竟于 1860 年和 1900 年两次被侵略北京的英法联军和八国联军烧毁，只剩下了一片废墟。

The most famous place of Beijing is exactly the Tian'anmen Square. Tian'anmen is the symbolization of the capital Beijing. The Gate Tower of Tian An Men is solemn and beautiful. The west of the square is the People's Great Hall, and the east is the National Museum of China. The south of the square is the Chairman Mao's Memorial. The center of the square is the Monument of the People's Heroes, and the adjacent Zhongnanhai is the seat of the Central Committee of the Communist Party of China and the State Council. Therefore we say that the Tian'anmen Square is the political center of the China's capital.

The most important street of Beijing is the Chang'an Avenue (the Everlasting Peace Street). The Everlasting Peace Street begins from the Fuxing Gate on the west, to the Jianguo Gate on the east. Its total length is 6 kilometers, and its width is 67 meters.

The most famous scenic spots and historic sites of Beijing are the Great Wall and the Imperial Palace (the Forbidden City). The Great Wall of China is located on the Badaling more than 70 kilometers to the northwest of Beijing city, and its total length is more than 6700 kilometers, across 6 provinces and cities in northern China. The Great Wall began to be built in the Warring States period. The present-day Great Wall was mostly built again in the Ming Dynasty, and it has been described as the miracle in the history of the world's architecture.

The Imperial Palace is the biggest and most complete existing imperial palace and ancient architecture complex in China, located in the center of Beijing city. It began to be built in the year of 1406, and it took 14 years to be finished. And 24 emperors of the two dynasties of Ming and Qing have lived in it.

The Summer Palace is situated in the northwest suburb of Beijing city, which is a beautiful royal garden and the largest existing imperial garden of ancient China.

The Old Summer Palace was originally the largest imperial garden of China, once called as the garden of all gardens. Unfortunately, this famous garden in the world was twice burnt away by the British and French Joined Forces and the Eight-Power Allied Forces respectively in the year of 1860 and 1900, and there was nothing

十三陵位于北京北部 40 多公里处，是明代十三位皇帝的陵墓，地面建筑宏伟，并建有巨大的地下宫殿。目前，十三陵可供参观的只有长陵和定陵。长陵是明成祖朱棣的陵墓，定陵是明神宗朱翊钧的陵墓。

天坛位于北京城南，是现存的中国最大的坛庙建筑，已有近 600 年的历史，是明、清两代皇帝祭天的地方。

琉璃厂，是一条古文化街，那里出售中国字画和文房四宝。中国特有的文书工具，即笔、墨、纸、砚，被誉为"文房四宝"。

雍和宫，是北京最大的喇嘛庙。

北海公园，是位于北京市中心的皇家公园。

此外，北京的旅游景点还有：香山公园（卧佛寺、碧云寺）、大观园、潭柘寺、大钟寺、白云观、北京猿人遗址、亚运村。

二、西安

西安在明朝之前称为"长安"。在这里以及附近建都的朝代共有 10 个：西周、秦、西汉、前赵、前秦、后秦、西魏、北周、隋朝和唐朝。

but ruins.

The Ming Tombs are located more than 40 kilometers north of Beijing, and they are the tombs of the thirteen emperors of the Ming Dynasty. The ground buildings are grand, while the underground ones are huge. At present, only the Long Mausoleum and the Stable Mausoleum are available for visiting. The Long Mausoleum is the mausoleum of Zhu Di, Emperor Chengzu of Ming Dynasty, and the Stable Mausoleum is the mausoleum of Zhu Yijun, Emperor Shenzong of Ming Dynasty.

The Temple of Heaven is located in the south of Beijing, which is the largest existing altar-temple architecture in China. It has already had a history of nearly 600 years, and it was the place where the emperors offered sacrifice to heaven in the dynasties of Ming and Qing.

Liulichang is an ancient cultural street, and the Chinese calligraphy and paintings and the Four Treasures of the Study are sold here. The China's peculiar writing instruments including the pen, the ink, the paper and the inkstone, are known as the Four Treasures of the Study.

The Yonghe Temple is the largest Lama Temple in Beijing.

The Beihai Park is the royal park located in the center of the Beijing city.

In addition, there are other touring attractions in Beijing such as the Fragrant Hill Park (the Temple of Reclining Buddha, the Temple of the Azure Clouds), the Grand View Garden, the Temple of Pool and the Wild Mulberry, the Big Bell Temple, the White Cloud Temple, the Site of Peking Man and the Asian Sports Village.

二、Xi'an

Xi'an was called as Chang'an before the Ming Dynasty. There were ten dynasties that built their capitals here and around here, including the West Zhou Dynasty, the Qin Dynasty, the Western Han Dynasty, the Former Zhao Dynasty, the Former Qin Dynasty, the Later Qin Dynasty, the Western Wei Dynasty, the Northern Zhou Dynasty, the Sui Dynasty and the Tang Dynasty.

西安的名胜古迹有：半坡博物馆（六七千年之前母系氏族公社一个村落的遗址）、秦始皇兵马俑、华清宫、秦陵、汉陵（汉武帝的茂陵）、唐陵（唐太宗的昭陵）、西安碑林、大雁塔、小雁塔（唐玄奘从印度取经回来译经的地方）、西安事变故址华清池。

三、济南

济南风光可以用下面的话来描述："四面荷花三面柳，一城山色半城湖。"——湖水的四周都是荷花，三面垂着杨柳；一城的美丽山色，有半城映照在湖水中。上面的话是一副对联（楹联），不是古诗句。它描写的是大明湖的美丽风光。

济南，是中国环渤海地区南翼和黄河中下游地区的中心城市，国家重要的政治、军事、文化中心，区域性金融中心，副省级城市，山东省省会。济南历史文化底蕴深厚，有着2700余年的历史，素有"天下泉城""世界泉水之都"的美誉，是象征中华文明重要起源的史前文明——龙山文化的发祥地和发现地，国家历史文化名城、国家创新型城市、中国软件名城、全国重要的交通枢纽和物流中心。继济南全运会取得圆满成功后，2013年济南举办了第十届中国艺术节，并成为2015年"第二十二届国际历史科学大会"的主办城市，为将济南加速建设成国际化大都市注入了新的活力。

The scenic spots and historic sites of Xi'an are as follows: the Banpo Museum (the site of a village of the matriarchal clan commune six-seven thousand years ago), the Qin Shihuang's Terracotta Warriors, the Hall of Glorious Purity (Hua Qing Palace), the Mausoleum of the First Qin Emperor, the Mausoleum of the Han Emperor [the Mao (luxuriant) Mausoleum of the Emperor Wu of Han Dynasty], the Tombs of Tang Dynasty (the Zhaoling Mausoleum of Emperor Taizong of Tang Dynasty), the Stele Forest of Xi'an, the Greater Wild Goose Pagoda, the Lesser Wild Goose Pagoda (the place where Tang Xuanzang translated the Buddhist Scriptures after he carried the Buddhist Scriptures back from India) and the Old Site of the Xi'an Incident — the Huaqing Hot Spring.

三、Ji' nan

The scenery of Jinan can be described with the following sentences — around the lake are lotuses, and on the three sides with weeping willows; a city of beautiful mountain scenery, half of which is reflected in the lake water. The above sentences are a couplet (distich), not two ancient verses, which describe the beautiful scenery of Daming Lake.

Jinan is the central city on the south wing of Circum-Bohai Sea Region and in the middle and lower reaches of the Yellow River region, which is the important national center of politics, military affairs and culture, the regional financial center, the sub-provincial city and the capital of Shandong province. In possession of profound historical and cultural deposits, with a history of more than 2700 years old, Jinan enjoys the fames as "the Spring City in the World" and "the Capital of Spring in the World". It is the birthplace cradle and the discovery site of the Longshan Culture, a prehistoric civilization that symbolizes the important origin of the Chinese civilization, which is also the famous city of the national history and culture, the national innovative city, a renowned software city in China, the important transportation hub and logistic center throughout the country. After the Jinan National Athletic Meet achieved the complete success, Jinan held the Tenth China

趵突泉公园——Spouting Spring（趵：spring forth；突：bulge）

趵突泉公园位于济南市中心区，南靠千佛山，东临泉城广场，北望大明湖，是以泉为主的特色园林，园内名泉众多。趵突泉位居"济南七十二名泉"之首，被誉为"天下第一泉"，也是最早见于古代文献的济南名泉。

趵突腾空——Spouting to the Sky

趵突腾空，明清时期位列"济南八景"之首，是对趵突泉喷涌盛况的生动描写。"三尺不消平地雪，四时长吼半空雷"等诗句生动地描绘了趵突泉喷涌的壮阔景象。

大明湖——Daming Lake

大明湖是天然湖泊，位于泉城特色风貌带的核心地区，因地处繁华都市之中而十分罕见，更因为由泉水汇集而成，在全国独一无二。景区占地面积103.4公顷，其中湖面57.7公顷。这里名胜荟萃，风景秀丽，素有"泉城明珠"的美誉。

明湖泛舟——Boating on the Daming Lake

船是大明湖的魂。在大明湖各式各样的游船中，最有韵味的当属古色古香的画船。无论是风和日丽，还是烟雨蒙蒙，乘坐在画船中，荡于一湖烟波之上，那情那景令人魂牵梦绕。

千佛山——Thousand-Buddha Mountain

千佛山古称历山，亦名舜耕山。相传上古虞舜帝为民时，曾躬耕于历山之下，故称舜耕山。据史料记载：隋朝年间，山东佛教盛行，虔诚的教徒依

Arts Festival in 2013, and became the host city of the Twenty-Second International Congress of Historical Science in 2015, which has injected the new vitality into the accelerating construction of international metropolis of Jinan.

Spouting Spring Park is located in the central district of Jinan, close to the Thousand-Buddha Mountain to the south, near the Spring City Plaza to the east, looking over the Daming Lake to the north, which is the characteristic garden dominated by the springs. There are a lot of famous springs in the garden. The Spouting Spring stands first among the seventy-two famous springs in Jinan, which is honored as the First Spring in the World, and also the famous spring of Jinan that was earliest recorded in ancient literature.

The Spouting to the Sky stood first among the eight sights of Jinan in the period of Ming and Qing Dynasty, which is the vivid description of the spectacle of the spouting of the Spouting Spring. Such verses as " No less than three inches like the snow on the flat ground, often roars at four seasons like the thunderclap in the air" and so on fully praise the magnificent sight of the Spouting Spring's spewing.

The Daming Lake is the natural lake, located in the central district of the Spring City characteristic landscape belt. It is rare because of its location in the busy city, also for its assembling by the spring water, which is unique in the whole country. The scenic area covers an acreage of 103.4 hectares, in which the lake surface covers 57.7 hectares. Here the scenic spots gather together; the scenery is beautiful; and it has been known as the Bright Pearl of the Spring City.

The Boat is the soul of the Daming Lake. Among all the kinds of pleasure-boats on the Daming Lake, the most lasting appeal should be the antique painting boat. Whether the wind is mild and the sun is bright, or it is in misty rain, to ride in the painting boat, and to loiter in the mist and the ripples of the lake, the feeling and the scenery can make people into haunting dreams.

The Thousand-Buddha Mountain was called as Li Mountain in ancient time, and also named as Shun Plow Mountain. According to the legend, in palaeoid, when the Emperor Yushun was a civilian, he once plowed under the Li Mountain, so it was

山沿壁镌刻了为数较多的石佛，因建千佛寺而得名千佛山。

泉城广场——Spring City Square

泉城广场是济南的中心广场，是国内首家被命名为"国际艺术广场"的城市广场，也是中国迄今为止唯一获得这一殊荣的广场设施。泉城广场地处山、泉、河、城怀抱之中，是市民休憩盘桓之胜地。

四、上海

上海简称沪或申，是中西文化的交汇点，形成了自己独特的文化意蕴和民俗风情，是一个被称为"魔都"的地方。在这里，东西方文化互相交融，外滩的西洋建筑与浦东的摩天大厦交相辉映；新天地既保留了昔日的石库门、老洋房，又展示着新的流行元素；南京路、淮海路、徐家汇商业城、豫园商城是上海的购物中心；躲藏在小剧院中的滑稽戏、独角戏、沪剧，还有如今的海派清口让人笑翻天；老饭店内的地道本帮菜、红房子的正宗法国大菜、城隍庙的小吃都是远近闻名，老街弄堂还能寻到古色古香的茶馆，衡山路的洋房中也有各种给人惊喜的酒吧。

上海市区有许多著名的旅游景点。

外滩：又名中山东一路，北起外白渡桥，南到金陵东路，全长约 1.5 公里，东临黄浦江，而西面是风格各异的大厦，有古典式、哥特式、罗马式、巴洛克式、文艺复兴式、东西合璧式等共 52 栋建筑，为上海的象征之一。

called Shun Plow Mountian. According to the record of history, in the Sui Dynasty, the Buddhism prevailed in Shandong, and the devout buddhists engraved numerous stone buddhas on the cliffs along the mountain, and built the Thousand-Buddha Temple. That's why the name of the Thousand-Buddha Mountain came into being.

The Spring City Square is the central plaza of Jinan, and the first urban square that has been named "the International Art Square " in china, also the only square facility that has won the laurel up to now in China. The Spring City Square is located in the embrace of the mountains, springs, rivers and city, which is the resort where the citizens can have a rest and stroll.

四、Shanghai

Shanghai, referred to as Hu or Shen for short, is the meeting point of Chinese and western cultures, having formed its own unique cultural implication and folk customs, a place called the Magic City. The eastern and western cultures blend with each other here, and the western architectures of the Bund and the skyscrapers of Pudong add radiance and beauty to each other. New Heaven and Earth of Shanghai not only retains the old Shanghai Gates and the old foreign-style houses, but also shows the new popular elements. Nanjing Road, Huaihai Road, Xujiahui Commercial District and Yuyuan Tourist Mart are the shopping centers of Shanghai. The Low Comedy, One-man Show, Shanghai Opera hidden in the small theaters and today's Shanghai Qing Mouth can make people laugh hilariously. The authentic local foods in the old restaurants, the authentic French dishes and the snacks in the Town God's Temple are all known far and wide. An antique teahouse can be found in some old street alley, and there are also a variety of surprising pubs in the foreign-style houses on Hengshan Road.

There are many famous tourist attractions in Shanghai.

The Bund, also known as Zhongshan East First Road, starts from the Waibaidu Bridge in the north, and ends at the Jinling East Road in the south. The total length is about 1.5 kilometers. It faces the Huangpu River in the east, and in the west the

南京路：东起外滩中山东一路，西至延安西路，全长5.5公里；以西藏中路为界分为东、西两段。南京东路辟为步行街，被誉为"中华商业第一街"。

豫园：位于福佑路、安仁街交界处，占地30余亩，始建于明嘉靖三十八年（1559年），距今有400多年的历史。园内有亭台楼阁、假山池沼，共有48处景点，景致各异。

浦东新区：位于黄浦江以东，长江口西南，面积523平方公里。在这里可以欣赏一批现代化功能性建筑等都市风景，如东方明珠电视塔、金茂大厦、杨浦江大桥、南浦大桥、奉浦大桥、徐浦大桥、浦东国际机场、滨江大道、世纪大道、中央公园等都市景观。

东方明珠电视塔：坐落于黄浦江畔浦东陆家嘴嘴尖上，与外滩隔江相望；东方明珠塔高468米，总建筑面积7.9万平方米，与左右两侧的南浦大桥、杨浦大桥一起形成双龙戏珠之势，成为上海改革开放的象征。

金茂大厦：位于浦东新区陆家嘴金融贸易区，大厦共88层，高420.5米，单体建筑面积达29万平方米，是中国传统建筑风格与世界高新技术的完美结合。设在88层的观光大厅，建筑面积1,520平方米。在此登高远眺，大上海的景观尽收眼底。

buildings of different styles, including fifty-two buildings of Classical style, Gothic style, Romanesque style, Baroque style, Renaissance style and the Combination of East-West style and so forth, forming one of the symbols of Shanghai.

Nanjing Road starts from the Bund, namely, Zhongshan East First Road, and ends at Yan'an West Road in the west, with a total length of 5.5 kilometers. It is divided into the two sections — the east section and the west section, taking Tibet Central Road as the boundary. The Nanjing East Road is designated as the pedestrian street and known as the First Street of Chinese Commerce.

Yuyuan Garden is located at the junction of Fuyou Road and Anren Street, covering an area of more than thirty acres. It was bulit in the thirty-eighth year of the reign of Emperor Jiaqing of the Ming Dynasty (1559), and has a history of more than 400 years. There are many pavilions, towers, rockeries and ponds in the garden, a total of 48 scenic spots with different sceneries.

Pudong New Area is located at the east of the Huangpu River and southwest of the Yangtze River estuary, covering an area of 523 square kilometers, where you can enjoy a number of modern functional buildings and other urban landscapes, such as the Oriental Pearl TV Tower, Jinmao Tower, Yangpu River Bridge, Nanpu Bridge, Fengpu Bridge, Xupu Bridge, Pudong International Airport, Riverside Avenue, Century Avenue and Central Park and others.

The Oriental Pearl TV Tower is located at the mouth of Lujiazui, Pudong, on the bank of the Huangpu River, facing the Bund across the river. The Oriental Pearl TV Tower is 468 meters high, with a total building area of 79,000 square meters. Together with the Nanpu Bridge and Yangpu Bridge on the left and right, it forms the momentum of two dragons playing with pearls and becomes the symbol of Shanghai's reform and opening up.

Jinmao Tower is located in the Lujiazui Financial and Trade Zone of Pudong New Area. The building has a total of 88 stories, and is 420.5 meters high, with a single building area of 290,000 square meters. It is the perfect combination of the Chinese traditional architecture style and the new high-tech in the world. The

中共一大会址：中国共产党第一次全国代表大会会址，是中国共产党的诞生地，位于兴业路 76 号（原望志路 106 号），是出席中共"一大"的上海代表李汉俊之兄李书城的住所，为一座具有 20 世纪 20 年代上海民居风格的石库门式楼房。纪念馆内还辟有三个陈列室，展出中国共产党创立时期的史迹和文物。

文庙：坐落在文庙路 215 号，是上海中心城区唯一的儒学圣地，著名的名胜古迹之一。它有 700 多年的历史，始建于元朝至元 31 年（1294 年），此后几经迁移，至清咸丰 5 年（1855 年）重建于今址。2002 年被公布为"上海市文物保护单位"。

三山会馆：位于上海市南浦大桥桥堍中山南路 1551 号，是上海唯一保存完好的晚清会馆建筑。始建于 1909 年，由福建旅沪水果商人集资兴建，因福州城内有三座山：东南于山、西南乌石山（亦称道山）、北面越王山（亦称闽山），故由此得名"三山"。会馆主体建筑占地 1,000 平方米，整幢建筑雕梁画栋、殿宇高大、别致秀丽，富有福建特色。三山会馆不仅具有很高的艺术欣赏价值，而且它还是上海市唯一保存完好的上海工人三次武装起义的遗址。

sightseeing hall on the eighty-eighth floor has a building area of 1,520 square meters, while looking afar from here, you can get a panoramic view of the great Shanghai.

The Site of the First National Congress of the Communist Party of China: the birthplace of the Communist Party of China, located at No.76, Xingye Road (No.106, Wangzhi Road, originally), was the residence of Li Shucheng, the elder brother of Li Hanjun, a Shanghai delegate to the First National Congress of the Communist Party of China, which is a Shikumen building with the residential style of Shanghai in the 1920s. The museum has three showrooms displaying the historical and cultural relics during the founding period of the Communist Party of China.

Confucian Temple is located in No.215, Confucian Temple Road, the only Confucian holy land in the central area of Shanghai, and one of the famous scenic spots and historical sites. It has a history of more than 700 years, and was built in the thirty-first year of Emperor Zhiyuan of the Yuan Dynasty (1294). After several migrations, it was rebuilt on today's site in the fifth year of Emperor Xianfeng (1855). It was announced as the Shanghai Cultural Relics Protection Unit in the year of 2002.

Three Mountain Guild Hall, located on the bridgehead of the Nanpu Bridge, No.1551, Zhongshan South Road, Shanghai, is the only well preserved guild hall architecture of the late Qing Dynasty in Shanghai. It was built in the year of 1909 by the fruit merchants in Shanghai from Fujian Province who raised the fund. Because there were three mountains within the Fuzhou city: Yu Mountain in the southeast, Black Stone Mountain(also called as Dao Mountain) in the southwest and Yue King Mountain (also known as Min Mountain) in the north, it was named the Three Mountains. The main building of the guild hall covers an area of 1,000 square meters, and the whole building abounds with carved beams and painted rafters. The shrine building is high, chic and beautiful, full of Fujian characteristics. The Three Mountain Guild Hall is not only of high artistic appreciation value, but also the only well-preserved site of the three armed insurrections of Shanghai

思考题：

中国有哪九大旅游区？各个旅游区有哪些旅游景点？

workers in the city.

Thinking Question:

What are the nine major tourist areas? And what tourist attractions are there in each tourist area?

第八章　中国的国际交往

中国的国际交往有着悠久的历史。早在西汉时期，中国就通过"丝绸之路"与中亚、西亚及欧洲一些国家开展了丝绸等方面的贸易交流。隋唐时期，唐玄奘去印度取经，鉴真和尚东渡日本传播佛学。明朝时期，政府曾经派遣郑和七次下西洋，先后到过亚洲和非洲等 30 多个国家。

第一节　中国的外交关系

20 世纪 50 年代，中国与苏联建立了友好联盟。

20 世纪 60 年代，中国与苏联的关系出现破裂，重点发展了与亚非拉"第三世界"国家的关系。

1971 年 10 月，中华人民共和国恢复了联合国的合法席位，外交上取得了一个重大胜利。

1972 年 2 月，美国总统尼克松访华，中美两国政府发表了《中美联合公报》，美国承认世界上只有一个中国，中华人民共和国政府是中国的唯一合

Chapter 8   China's International Contacts

The Chinese international Contacts have a long history. As early as in the period of the Western Han Dynasty, China traded and communicated on silk and other aspects with the Central Asia, West Asia and some European countries through the Silk Road. In the periods of the Sui and the Tang Dynasty, Tang Xuanzang went to India for the Buddhist Scriptures, and the Monk Jianzhen went east to Japan to spread Buddhism. In the period of Ming Dynasty, the government once sent Zheng He to the Western seas seven times, who had successively been to more than 30 countries in Asia and Africa.

Section 1   China's Diplomatic Relations

In 1950s, China established the friendly alliance with the Soviet Union.

In 1960s, while the relations between China and the Soviet Union ruptured, China put emphasis upon developing relations with the third world countries of Asia, Africa and Latin America.

In Oct. of 1971, the People's Republic of China resumed the legitimate seat at the United Nations, and had achieved a great victory on diplomacy.

In Feb. of 1972, the United States President Richard Nixon visited China, and the *Sino–US Joint Communiqué* was issued. The U.S. acknowledged that there was

法政府。从此，中美两国结束了对立状态。

1979 年 1 月 28 日至 2 月 5 日，中国国务院副总理邓小平对美国进行正式访问。

1979 年，中美两国建立了正式的外交关系。

根据中华人民共和国外交部官网的统计资料，截至 2019 年 3 月，中国已经与世界上 178 个国家建立了外交关系。

第二节　中国的文化交流

改革开放 40 多年来，尤其是党的十八大以来，我国对外文化交流传播工作取得了丰硕成果。

据统计，近年来我国的对外文化交流项目的年均总数与受众人次均超过改革开放前 30 年的总和。截至 2017 年年底，我国已与 157 个国家签署了文化合作协定，累计签署文化交流执行计划近 800 个，初步形成了覆盖世界主要国家和地区的政府间文化交流与合作网络。党的十八大以来，我国已在五大洲举办了 30 余次大型中国文化年（节）系列活动，中俄、中美、中欧、中阿、中非等文化交流合作机制向更高层次发展。

only one China in the world, and the Government of the People's Republic of China was the sole legal Government of China. Since then, China and the United States have ended their antagonism.

From Jan. 28th to February 5th, 1979, Deng Xiaoping , the Vice Premier of the State Council of China, paid an official visit to the United States.

In 1979, the two countries — China and the United States established the formal diplomatic relations.

According to the statistical data from the official website of the Ministry of Foreign Affairs of the People's Republic of China, up to March 2019, China had established diplomatic relations with 178 countries in the world.

Section 2 China's Cultural Exchanges

Over the past 40 years, especially since the 18th National Congress of the Communist Party of China, China has achieved fruitful results in the cultural exchanges and communications with other countries.

According to statistics in recent years, China's average annual total number of foreign cultural exchange programs and the number of audiences are both more than the sum of the 30 years before the reform and opening up. As of the end of 2017, China had signed cultural cooperation agreements with 157 countries, and cumulatively signed nearly 800 cultural exchange execution plans. At the same time, a network of inter-governmental cultural exchanges and cooperation covering the world's major countries and regions had taken shape. Since the 18th National Congress of the Communist Party of China, more than 30 large-scale Chinese Culture Year (Festival) series of activities had been held in the five continents. The Sino-Russian, Sino-American, Sino-European, Sino-Arab, Sino-African cultural exchange and cooperation mechanisms are developing to a higher level.

借助一系列文化活动、海外中国文化中心、孔子学院等平台，中国杂技、武术、书法、京剧、太极拳等传统文化纷纷走上国际舞台。通过一系列"文化年""国家年""交流年"等大型的国际文化交流活动，中国的对外文化交流已经形成许多著名品牌。"欢乐春节""东亚文化之都""中非文化聚焦""拉美艺术季""相约北京"等国际性文化节庆、赛事和展会品牌不断涌现，成为广泛传播中华文化的重要平台。

2017 年"欢乐春节"活动在全球 140 个国家和地区的 500 多座城市举办了 2000 多场活动，海外受众突破 2.8 亿人次，近 20 个语种的上千家国际主流媒体进行了密集报道，覆盖受众近 30 亿人，影响遍及全球，成为向世界各国展示中华文化魅力的重要平台。在全球很多地方，春节已成为本土化的节日。芬兰赫尔辛基市市长曾表示："春节已经成为赫尔辛基全体市民的节日。"

海外中国文化中心备受欢迎。截至 2017 年，海外中国文化中心开展各类文化活动达 4000 余场次，直接受众达到 800 余万人次，成为全方位展示中华文化精粹和国家形象的重要平台。到 2020 年，海外中国文化中心总数将达到 50 个，形成覆盖全球主要国家和地区的中国文化对外传播推广网络。

孔子学院以语言为媒，架起了各国人民相遇相知的桥梁。2004 年，全球第一所孔子学院在韩国汉城揭牌。截至 2017 年 12 月 31 日，146 个国家（地区）建立 525 所孔子学院和 1113 个孔子课堂，为增进中外人民的相互了解

With the aid of a series of cultural activities, Overseas Chinese Cultural Centers, and Confucius Institutes and other platforms, Chinese acrobatics, martial arts, calligraphy, Peking opera, shadowboxing and other traditional cultures have stepped onto the international stage one after another. Through a series of large-scale international cultural exchange activities, such as the Cultural Year, the National Year, the Exchange Year and others, China has formed many famous brands in the foreign cultural exchanges. The brands of international cultural festivals, events and exhibitions, such as Happy Chinese New Year, the Capital of East Asian Culture, Sino-African Culture Focus, Latin American Art Season, Meeting in Beijing and others have kept emerging, and become an important carrier for spreading Chinese culture widely.

In 2017, more than 2000 Happy Chinese New Year activities were held in more than 500 cities in the 140 countries and regions around the world, whose overseas audiences exceeded 280 million person-times, of which more than one thousand international mainstream media in nearly 20 languages provided intensive coverage, covering nearly 3 billion audiences. With the global influence, Happy Chinese New Year has become an important platform to show the charm of Chinese culture to all the countries around the world. In many parts of the world, the Spring Festival has become a local festival. The mayor of Helsinki, Finland once said: "The Spring Festival has become a festival for all the citizens of Helsinki."

The Overseas Chinese Cultural Centers have enjoyed great popularity. Up to 2017, the Overseas Chinese Cultural Centers had held more than 4000 various cultural activities whose direct audiences had reached up to more than 8 million person-times, and had become important platforms to display the essence of the Chinese culture and national image in an all-round way. By 2020, the total number of the Overseas Chinese Cultural Centers will reach 50, forming a network for the dissemination and promotion of the Chinese culture in major countries and regions around the world.

With languages as the medium, Confucius Institutes have built a bridge for people of all countries to meet and know each other. In 2004, the world's first Confucius Institute was unveiled the nameplate in Seoul, South Korea. As of

和友谊，为促进人类文明的交流互鉴发挥了独特作用。

"一带一路"建设，为多样文化交汇相通注入了动力。过去5年多来，通过"丝绸之路国际艺术节""海上丝绸之路国际艺术节""丝绸之路（敦煌）国际文化博览会"等平台，以及"丝绸之路国际剧院联盟""丝绸之路国际博物馆联盟""丝绸之路国际艺术节联盟"等交流与合作机制，夯实了"一带一路"建设的民意与社会基础。

此外，国际文化交流中的一项重要内容就是电影交流。国际上的重要电影节，中国一般都会参加，并且已经有80多部电影在国际电影节上获奖。

电影《黄土地》1985年获得第38届洛迦诺国际电影节银豹奖和天主教人道精神奖。

电影《归来》2014年4月17日入围第67届戛纳国际电影节，2014年7月23日入选第39届多伦多国际电影节。

第三节　"一带一路"——发展倡议

"一带一路"是"丝绸之路经济带"和"21世纪海上丝绸之路"的简称，

December 31st, 2017, 525 Confucius Institutes and 1113 Confucius Classrooms had been established in 146 countries and regions, playing a unique role in enhancing the understanding and friendship between Chinese and foreign people, and promoting exchanges and mutual learning between human civilizations.

The construction of "One Belt and One Road" has injected impetus for the interconnection and communication of diverse cultures. Over the past five years, through the platforms such as the Silk Road International Art Festival, the Maritime Silk Road International Art Festival, the Silk Road (Dunhuang) International Cultural Exposition and so on, and the communication and cooperation mechanisms such as the Silk Road International Theater Federation, the Silk Road International Federation of Museums, the Silk Road International Art Festival Alliance and so forth, the public opinion and social foundation of the One Belt and One Road Construction have been consolidated.

In addition, an important content in international cultural exchange is exactly the movie exchange. Generally China will participate in important international movie festivals, and there already have been more than eighty films that have won awards in international film festivals.

The film *Yellow Land* in 1985, won the Silver Leopard Award and the Catholic Humanitarian Award at the Thirty-eighth Locarno International Film Festival.

The movie *Coming Back* was shortlisted for the 67th Cannes International Film Festival on April 17th, 2014, and was selected for the 39th Toronto International Film Festival on 23rd July, 2014.

Section 3 One Belt and One Road— Development Initiative

"One Belt and One Road" is short for the Silk Road Economic Belt and the

目的是积极发展与沿线国家的经济合作伙伴关系。

2015 年 3 月 28 日，国家发展改革委员会、外交部、商务部联合发布了《推动共建丝绸之路经济带和 21 世纪海上丝绸之路的愿景与行动》。

2017 年 5 月 14 日至 5 月 15 日，"一带一路"国际合作高峰论坛在北京举行，习近平主席出席高峰论坛开幕式，并主持领导人圆桌峰会。

启动原则："一带一路"建设秉承的是共商、共建、共享原则。

启动目的：在通路、通航的基础上通商，形成和平与发展的新常态。

一带一路的版图：

"一带"指的是"丝绸之路经济带"，是在陆地。它有三个走向，从中国出发，一是经中亚、俄罗斯到达欧洲；二是经中亚、西亚至波斯湾、地中海；三是中国到东南亚、南亚、印度洋。"一路"指的是"21 世纪海上丝绸之路"。重点方向是两条：一是从中国沿海港口过南海到印度洋，延伸至欧洲；二是从中国沿海港口过南海到南太平洋。

丝路新图：

1. 北线 A

北美洲（美国，加拿大）—北太平洋—日本，韩国—日本海—扎鲁比诺港（海参崴，斯拉夫扬卡等）—珲春—延吉—吉林—长春—蒙古国—俄罗斯—欧洲

21st Century Maritime Silk Road, whose aim is to actively develop the economic and cooperative fellowship with the countries along the belt and road.

On the 28th, March, 2015, the National Development and Reform Commission, the Ministry of Foreign Affairs and the Ministry of Commerce jointly issued the *Vision and Action to Promote Co-Constructing the Silk Road Economic Belt and the 21st Century Maritime Silk Road*.

On May 14th to 15th, 2017, the One Belt and One Road International Cooperation Peak Forum was held in Beijing. President Xi Jinping attended the opening ceremony of the Peak BBS and hosted the leaders' roundtable summit.

The Starting Principles are as follows: The construction of One Belt and One Road is based on the principles of co-consulting, co-constructing and co-sharing.

The starting purpose is as follows: Trade should be conducted on the basis of access to roads and navigations, so that the new normal of peace and development will be formed.

The Layout of Belt and Road Initiative:

"One Belt" refers to the "Silk Road Economic Belt", which is on the land. It has three trends. Departing from China, the first route is through the Central Asia and Russia to Europe. The second route is through the Central Asia and the Western Asia to the Persian Gulf and the Mediterranean Sea. And the third route is from China to the Southeast Asia, the Southern Asia and the Indian Ocean. "One Road" refers to the "Twenty-First Century Maritime Silk Road". There are two key directions: One is from China's coastal ports across the South China Sea to the Indian Ocean , extending to Europe, and the other is from China's coastal ports through the South China Sea to the South Pacific.

The New Map of the Silk Road is as follows:

1. The Northern Line A

The North America (the United States, Canada)—The North Pacific—Japan, the South Korea—The Sea of Japan—Zarubino Port (Vladivostok, Slavyanka, etc.)— Huichun—Yanji—Jilin—Changchun—Mongolia—Russia—Europe

2. 北线 B

北京—俄罗斯—德国—北欧

3. 中线：

北京—西安—乌鲁木齐—阿富汗—哈萨克斯坦—匈牙利—巴黎

4. 南线

泉州—福州—广州—海口—北海—河内—吉隆坡—雅加达—科伦坡—加尔各答—内罗毕—雅典—威尼斯

5. 中心线

连云港—郑州—西安—兰州—新疆—中亚—欧洲

项目落地：

肯尼亚是中国"一带一路"倡议在非洲唯一的支点，是新丝路建设中获得中国资金援助最多的国家。

2014 年 5 月，李克强总理访问肯尼亚期间，中肯签署了关于蒙巴萨—内罗毕铁路相关合作协议。蒙内铁路是肯尼亚百年来建设的首条新铁路，是东非铁路网的"咽喉"，也是东非次区域互联互通重大项目。东非铁路规划全长 2700 公里，预计总造价 250 亿美元。

2015 年 7 月 1 日至 7 月 3 日，在东非肯雅塔国际会议中心（KICC）举办了肯尼亚—中国贸易周，200 多家中国企业集中展示了自己的产品。

思考题：

阐释中国"一带一路"发展倡议的原则和目的。

2. The Northern Line B

Beijing—Russia—Germany—The Northern Europe

3. The Middle Line

Beijing—Xi'an—Urumqi—Afghanistan—Kazakhstan—Hungary—Paris

4. The Southern Line

Quanzhou—Fuzhou—Guangzhou—Haikou—The North Sea—Hanoi—Kuala Lumpur—Djakarta—Colombo—Calcutta—Nairobi—Athens—Venice

5. The Central Line

Lianyungang—Zhengzhou—Xi'an—Lanzhou—Xinjiang—the Central Asia—Europe

Project Landing:

Kenya is the only pivot point for China's One Belt and One Road Initiative in Africa, which has received from China the largest amount of financial assistance in construction of the new Silk Road.

During the visit of the Premier Li Keqiang to Kenya in May, 2014, China and Kenya signed a cooperation agreement on the Mombasa-Nairobi Railway. The Mombasa-Nairobi Railway is the first new railway to be built in Kenya for the last one hundred years, which is the throat of the East African railway network, also a major project of interconnectivity and interworking in the East Africa subregion. The East African Railway has been projected to be 2700 kilograms long, whose total cost is expected to be 25 billion U.S. dollars.

During July 1st to 3rd, 2015, the Kenyatta International Conference Center held the Kenya-China Trade Week in the International Exhibition Center in Kenya of the East Africa, where more than 200 Chinese companies concentrated on showing their products.

Thinking Question:

Expound the Starting principles and purpose of the "One Belt and One Road" development initiative of China.

第九章　中国人的气质

何为真正的中国人？这一直是一个广为探讨的话题。有一本书就叫作《中国人的精神》。《中国人的精神》又名《春秋大义》，此书是由国学大师辜鸿铭的一系列英文论文结集而成，是东西方文化比较的早期代表作品。辜鸿铭在书中把中国人同英国人、美国人、德国人、法国人进行比较，指出中国人同时具备深刻、博大、淳朴和文雅四种美德，主张用中国传统的儒家思想解决西方社会中存在的问题。

《中国人的精神》一书力图捍卫中国的传统文化。此书出版后在西方社会引起巨大反响，先后被译为德语、法语、日语、汉语等多种语言，并多次再版。德国因为此书而掀起数十年的"辜鸿铭热"。

辜鸿铭（1857年7月18日—1928年4月30日），英文名字Thomson。早年，辜鸿铭的祖辈由今福建省泉州市惠安县迁居南洋，并积累下丰厚的财产和声望。辜鸿铭出生于南洋马来半岛西北的槟榔屿（马来西亚的槟城州）一个英国人的橡胶园内。他的父亲辜紫云当时是英国人经营的一个橡胶园的总管，操一口流利的闽南话，能讲英语和马来语。他的母亲则是金发碧眼的

Chapter 9　The Temperaments of the Chinese People

What is the real Chinese person? This has always been a topic of great discussion. There is a book titled *The Spirit of the Chinese People*, which is also named *The Great Righteousness of Spring and Autumn*. It has been collected into a book from a series of English treatises by Gu Hongming, the great master of Chinese culture, and was the early representative work of the east-west cultural comparison. In the book, Gu Hongming compared the Chinese with the British, the American, the French and the German, pointing that the Chinese people had simultaneously four virtues of depth, broadness, simplicity and gentleness. And he advocated to solve the problems existing in the western society with the traditonal Chinese Confucianism.

The book *The Spirit of the Chinese People* was an attempt to defend the traditional Chinese culture, and after its publication, it caused a great repercussion in the western society. It has successively been translated into German, French, Japanese, Chinese and other languages, and has been republished many times. Because of this book, Germany once had a Gu Hongming fever lasting for decades.

Gu Hongming, was born in July 18th, 1857, and died in April 30th, 1928, with an English name Thomson. In the early years, Gu Hongming's ancestors emigrated to the Southeast Asia from Hui'an County, Quan Zhou City, Fu Jian Province, China, and accumulated rich property and prestige. Gu Hongming was born in an British rubber plantation in the northwest of the Malaya Peninsula in the Southeast Asia

西洋人，讲英语和葡萄牙语。当时的橡胶园园主布朗先生自己没有子女，非常喜欢他，将他收为义子，让他阅读莎士比亚、培根等人的作品。

1867 年，布朗夫妇返回英国时，把 10 岁的辜鸿铭带到了当时最强大的西方帝国。1870 年，14 岁的辜鸿铭被送往德国学习科学。后来他回到英国，并以优异的成绩被著名的爱丁堡大学录取。1877 年，辜鸿铭获得文学硕士学位，后又赴德国莱比锡大学等著名学府研究文学和哲学。此后，辜鸿铭获文、哲、理、神等 13 个博士学位，会 9 种语言。1880 年，辜鸿铭结束自己 14 年的求学历程返回故乡槟城。1885 年，辜鸿铭 28 岁，前往中国内地。1913 年，辜鸿铭和泰戈尔一起获诺贝尔文学奖提名。1915 年辜鸿铭在北京大学任教授，主讲英国文学。1928 年 4 月 30 日，辜鸿铭在北京病逝，享年 72 岁。

下面这篇文章是辜鸿铭对中国人的看法和对中国人精神的阐释。文章的题目就是《中国人的精神》。

中国人的精神（节选）

辜鸿铭

——在北京东方协会上宣读的一篇论文

首先，请允许我向大家解释一下今天下午我打算讨论的议题。这篇论

(present-day Penang of Malaysia). His father, Gu Ziyun who spoke fluent Minnan dialect, and could speak English and Malay , was the main steward of the rubber plantation owned by the British. His mother was a blond and blue-eyed westerner, speaking English and Portuguese. The then owner of the rubber plantation — Mr. Brown had no children of his own, and liked him very much, who took him as an adopted son, and led him read the works of Shakespeare, Bacon and others.

In the year of 1867, when Mr. and Mrs Brown returned to Britain, they brought the ten-year-old Gu Hongming to the most powerful western empire of the time. In 1870, the fourteen-year-old Gu Hongming was sent to Germany to study Science. Later, he returned to England with an excellent marks , and was admitted to the prestigious Edinburgh University. In 1877, Gu Hongming received a master's degree in literature. Later, he went to the Leipzig University in Germany and other famous universities to study literature and philosophy. During that time, Gu Hongming received 13 doctorates in literature, philosophy, science, theology and so on, and could speak 9 kinds of languages. In 1880, Gu Hongming returned to his hometown Penang, ending his own 14 years of schooling. In the year of 1885, Gu Hongming was 28 years old, and left for Chinese Mainland. In the year of 1913, along with Tagore, Gu Hongming was nominated for the Nobel Prize in literature. In the year of 1915, Gu Hongming worked as a professor at Peking University, teaching the English Literature. On the 30th April, 1928, Gu Hongming died of an illness, at the age of 72 years old.

The following article is Gu Hongming's view of the Chinese people and an explanation of the spirit of the Chinese people. And its title is exactly "The Spirit of the Chinese People" .

The Spirit of the Chinese People (Excerpts)

Gu Hongming

——A Paper that has been read before the Oriental Society of Peking

Let me first of all explain to you what I propose, with your permission, this

文的题目我把它叫做"中国人的精神"。在这里，我所说的"中国人的精神"并不仅仅意味着中国人的性格或者特征。此前，中国人的精神已经被做过很多描绘，但是，我想大家会同意我的看法——到目前为止，这种对中国人精神的描绘或者列举都没有给我们一个关于中国人内在本质的清晰轮廓。此外，当我们谈到中国人的性格或特征时，是不可能一概而论的。正如你所知道的，中国北方人的性格与中国南方人的性格是不同的，正如德国人的性格与意大利人的性格不同一样。

我所说的中国人的精神，指的是一种中国人赖以生存的精神，一种中国人在心灵、脾气、感情方面具有本质独特性的东西，这种东西使得中国人与其他所有人，特别是现代的欧洲人和美国人区别开来。或许，能够更准确地表达我的意思的最好方式是，把我们所讨论的主题叫做中国类型的人，或者用更加简洁的词语来说，就是，真正的中国人。

那么，什么是真正的中国人呢？我可以肯定，你们会同意我的观点，这是一个非常有趣的话题，尤其是在目前，当下的中国，从我们所看到的发生在我们身边的种种变化看来，似乎具有中国特性的人——真正的中国人——即将消失，取而代之的将会是一种新型的人类——进步的或者说是现代的中国人。实际上，我提议，在真正的中国人，也就是老式的中国人完全从这个世界上消失之前，我们应该再最后好好地看看他们，看看我们能不能从他们身上发现一些使得他们与其他的所有人，以及我们看到的当下中国正在出现的新型人如此不同的有机特质。

此时，我想，老式的中国人给你的第一印象就是他身上没有野蛮的、粗鲁的或者凶恶的东西。采纳一个用在动物身上的术语，我们可以说真正的中国人是一种驯养的物种。我想，你会同意我的观点——拿一个中国社会最底层的人来说，他身上的动物性比你在欧洲社会同样阶层的人身上所发现的要

afternoon to discuss. The subject of our paper I have called *"The Spirit of the Chinese People."* I do not mean here merely to speak of the character or characteristics of the Chinese people. Chinese characteristics have often been described before, but I think you will agree with me that such description or enumeration of the characteristics of the Chinese people hitherto have given us no picture at all of the inner being of the Chinaman. Besides, when we speak of the character or characteristics of the Chinese, it is not possible to generalize. The character of the Northern Chinese, as you know, is as different from that of the Southern Chinese as the character of the Germans is different from that of the Italians.

But what I mean by the spirit of the Chinese people, is the spirit by which the Chinese people live, something constitutionally distinctive in the mind, temper and sentiment of the Chinese people which distinguishes them from all other people,especially from those of modern Europe and America. Perhaps, I can best express what I mean by calling the subject of our discussion the Chinese type of humanity, or, to put it in plainer and shorter words, the real Chinaman.

Now, what is the real Chinaman? That, I am sure, you will all agree with me, is a very interesting subject, especially at the present moment, when from what we see going on around us in China today, it would seem that the Chinese type of humanity—the real Chinaman—is going to disappear and, in his place, we are going to have a new type of humanity—the progressive or modern Chinaman. In fact I propose that before the real Chinaman, the old Chinese type of humanity, disappears altogether from the world we should take a good last look at him and see if we can find anything organically distinctive in him which makes him so different from all other people and from the new type of humanity which we see rising up in China today.

Now the first thing, I think, which will strike you in the old Chinese type of humanity is that there is nothing wild, savage or ferocious in him. Using a term which is applied to animals, we may say of the real Chinaman that he is a domesticated creature. Take a man of the lowest class of the population in China

少得多——更少些野蛮动物的特性，也就是德国人所谓的"动物野性"。实际上，在我看来，有一个词可以概括中国人给你的印象，那就是英语单词"gentle"（温文尔雅）。但是，我使用温文尔雅这个词语并不意味着本性的软弱或者懦弱的服从。

已故的麦克格温博士说过："中国人的温顺并不是那种被阉割的、心碎的人的温顺。"我用"gentle"这个词意味着没有强硬，没有苛刻，没有粗暴，没有暴力，实际上，没有任何让你感觉不快的东西。在真正的中国人身上有一种气质，可以说是一种沉静的、清醒的、经过历练的成熟练达，就像你在一块冶炼适度的金属中看到的特质一样。确实，一个真正的中国人身体上和精神上的缺陷，如果不能被消除的话，至少可以被他身上这种温文尔雅的气质所淡化。

或许，真正的中国人是粗糙的，但粗糙中没有粗野；或许，真正的中国人是丑陋的，但丑陋中没有丑恶；或许，真正的中国人是粗俗的，但粗俗中没有霸气和嚣张；或许，真正的中国人是愚笨的，但愚笨中没有荒谬；或许，真正的中国人是圆通的，但圆通中没有恶意。其实，我想说的是，真正的中国人，即使是在他们身体上、思想上和性格上的缺点和缺陷里，也没有什么令人反感的东西。你很少能够找到一个绝对令人厌恶的真正的老派的中国人，即使是在社会最底层的人群里。

我想说的是，真正的中国人给你的总体印象是，他很文雅，一种难以言表的文雅。当你分析真正的中国人身上的这种难以言表的文雅特质时，你会发现它是两种东西结合的产物，即同情心和理解力。
……

最后，关于我们现在所讨论的主题——中国人的精神，或者什么是真正

and, I think, you will agree with me that there is less of animality in him, less of the wild animal, of what the Germans call "Rohheit", than you will find in a man of the same class in a European society. In fact, the one word, it seems to me, which will sum up the impression which the Chinese type of humanity makes upon you is the English word "gentle". By gentleness I do not mean softness of nature or weak submissiveness.

"The docility of the Chinese"says the late Dr. D. J. Macgowan, "is not the docility of a broken-hearted, emasculated people." But by the word "gentle" I mean absence of hardness, harshness, roughness, or violence, in fact of anything which jars upon you. There is in the true Chinese type of humanity an air, so to speak, of a quiet, sober, chastened mellowness, such as you find in a piece of well-tempered metal. Indeed the very physical and moral imperfections of a real Chinaman are, if not redeemed, at least softened by this quality of gentleness in him.

The real Chinaman may be coarse, but there is no grossness in his coarseness. The real Chinaman may be ugly, but there is no hideousness in his ugliness. The real Chinaman may be vulgar, but there is no aggressiveness, no blatancy in his vulgarity. The real Chinaman may be stupid, but there is no absurdity in his stupidity. The real Chinaman may be cunning, but there is no malignity in his cunning. In fact, what I want to say is, that even in the faults and blemishes of body, mind and character of the real Chinaman, there is nothing which revolts you. It is seldom that you will find a real Chinaman of the old school, even of the lowest type, who is positively repulsive.

I say that the total impression which the Chinese type of humanity makes upon you is that he is gentle, that he is inexpressibly gentle. When you analyse this quality of inexpressible gentleness in the real Chinaman, you will find that it is the product of a combination of two things, namely, sympathy and intelligence.

...

Finally, let me shortly sum up what I want to say on the subject of our

的中国人，我简短地概括一下我的观点。我已经向你们揭示过了，真正的中国人是一个过着成年人的理性的生活，同时又有着孩子般单纯心灵的人；中国人的精神是灵魂与理智的巧妙结合。

现在，如果你在中国人公认为优秀的艺术和文学作品中考查一下中国人的精神产物，你会发现，正是灵魂与智慧的巧妙结合，使得它们如此令人满足和愉悦。马修·阿诺德对荷马的诗歌所做的评论也同样适用于所有优秀的中国文学作品——"它不但具有深刻触动人类内在灵魂的力量，这一点是伏尔泰不能达到的，也是伏尔泰的弱点，而且它也以伏尔泰那种令人钦佩的朴素和理性表达了理解和领悟。"

思考题：

你怎么看待中国人？谈谈你对中国人的感受和看法。

present discussion—the Spirit of the Chinese People or what is the real Chinaman. The real Chinaman, I have shown you, is a man who lives the life of a man of adult reason with the simple heart of a child, and the spirit of the Chinese people is a happy union of soul and intellect.

Now if you examine the products of the Chinese mind in their standard works of art and literature, you will find that it is the happy union of soul with the intellect which makes them so satisfying and delightful. What Matthew Arnold says of the poetry of Homer is true of all Chinese standard literature, that " it has not only the power of profoundly touching that natural heart of humanity, which it is the weakness of Voltaire that he cannot reach, but can also address the understanding with all Voltaire's admirable simplicity and rationality.

Thinking Question:

How do you think of the Chinese People? Talk about your feelings and opinions about the Chinese people.

参考文献
Bibliography

［1］辜鸿铭. 中国人的精神［M］. 北京：北京燕山出版社，2009.

［2］郭鹏. 中国概况 China Panorama［M］. 北京：高等教育出版社，2012.

［3］黄发红，朱玥颖，李欣怡. 数说改革开放 40 年：中国对外文化交流取得丰硕成果［EB/OL］. (2018-10-29)［2018-11-30］. http://www.chinanews.com/gn/2018/ 10-29/8662256.shtml.

［4］金敬华，常庆丰. 看中国 谈文化（下册）［M］. 济南：山东友谊出版社，2013.

［5］莫海斌等. 中国概况［M］. 广州：暨南大学出版社，2012.

［6］人民网. 李克强访问肯尼亚 中国拿下东非铁路大单［EB/OL］. (2014-05-11)［2014-05-28］. http://politics.people.com.cn/n/2014/0511/c1001-25002425.html.

［7］宋业瑾，蔡涛. 看中国 谈文化（中册）［M］. 济南：山东友谊出版社，2013.

［8］王顺洪. 中国概况［M］. 北京：北京大学出版社，2003.

［9］温静 赵静. 复盘 60 年来中国电视剧发展史［EB/OL］. (2018-07-11)［2018-08-12］. https://www.sohu.com/a/240641980_351788.

［10］肖立. 中国概况教程［M］. 北京：北京大学出版社，2009.

［11］杨存田. 中国风俗概观［M］. 北京：北京大学出版社，1994.

［12］张捷鸿，张幼冬，郭文娟. 看中国 谈文化（上册）［M］. 济南：山东友谊出版社，2013.

［13］张英，金舒年. 中国传统文化与现代生活——留学生中级文化读本（1）［M］. 北京：北京大学出版社，2003.

［14］中华人民共和国国家统计局. 2010 年第六次全国人口普查主要数据公报（第 1 号）［EB/OL］. (2010-04-28)［2014-05-26］. http://politics.people.com.cn/GB/1026/14506836.html.

后记——致谢

Postscript-Acknowledgement

此书稿是我在山东交通学院国际教育学院从事留学生教学工作的结晶。在此书稿即将出版之际，我驻足回首，心存感激，感谢国际教育学院的诸位领导和同事。

首先，我要感谢国际教育学院的院长商岳先生。2014年春天，我如愿以偿调至国际教育学院从事对外汉语教学工作。我感受比较深刻的一点是商院长作为领导的素质之一——知人善用，用人所长。我记得在一次教学工作专题会议上，商院长号召大家要发挥自己的专长，做好自己的本职工作，然后就谈到了我，他说："比如李博士性情单纯，喜欢看书，那么，我就让你好好看书，好好备课，好好上课，把教学工作搞好；如果我让你做别的工作，比如招生工作，比如管理工作，可能过不了多久，你就烦了，就会想着离开。"接着，商院长还引用了那句俗语"此处不留爷，自有留爷处"。听了这句戏谑的话，大家都笑了起来。我也微笑着回答："不会的，商院！我不会干，还不会学嘛；我不会再到其他地方去了，此地是我教学职业生涯的最后一站了。"正是因为商院长善于用人之长，我才能够有一定的时间安心、安静地坐在书桌旁，心无旁骛地读书备课，才能够积累成这部书稿。借此新书出版之机，真诚感谢商院长！

当然，毋庸置疑，商院长作为一个领导还具有一个高水平领导的诸多素质——进取精神、实干精神、开拓精神、创新意识、开阔的视野、前瞻的眼界、包容的胸怀……正是因为商院长的个人素质和领导能力，国际教育学院才能够不断发展壮大、蓬勃向上。

其次，我要感谢国际教育学院的党总支书记刘永东先生。刘书记心胸坦荡敞亮、磊落豁达。记得，我刚来国际学院的时候，因为跟同事沟通不畅，颇感郁闷。有天下午，我下班后去乘坐班车的时候，刚好遇到刘书记，我就跟他一起边走边聊。他一番坦荡豁达的话语，使我的情绪变得轻松明亮起来。尤其是今年春天我在教学管理工作中遇到困难的时候，刘书记在周三的例会上光明磊落地肯定了我的用心，认可我的付出，支持我的工作。我还记得那天下午下班后，我提着学校工会发放的福利——一大桶花生油下楼的时候恰巧遇到刘书记，刘书记帮我提着那一大桶花生油一直走到班车的停车点。真诚感谢刘书记！

最后，我要感谢国际教育学院的副院长万征先生。万院长正直无私，平和淡泊。来国际教育学院之前，对于万院长我是久闻其名，但不甚了解。到国际教育学院之后，最初我跟万院长在一个办公室工作并受万院长的直接领导，才逐渐熟悉起来。万院长也同样是胸怀坦荡，光明磊落，正直无私，勤勉敬业，严谨认真，而且淡泊名利。

起初，我一直想当然地认为万院长在职称上已经是教授了。后来有一天，跟同事聊天的时候，无意中说起来，我才知道万院长还是副教授呢，不由心生感慨：万院长这么好的人品，这么好的学问，这么敬业，这么勤恳，这么严谨，这么认真，这么不计名利……他竟然还不是教授呢！那么，我作为副教授也不必为此感到羞愧了吧！因为万院长的淡泊名利，所以，我才能够拥有释然坦然的心境。

一天午后，我和闺蜜在回办公室的路上说起万院长。她说："跟万院长这样的人一起共事会很安心、很放心、很开心。"我说："我举手同意。"她又说："如果社会上像万院长这样的人增加一个，那么，整个社会的幸福指数就会提高一分！"我说："我举双手同意。"感谢万院长。

感谢国际教育学院的副院长刘春光博士。刘院长品行端正，尊重领导，团结同志，工作勤勉，作风踏实，上任以来一直大力支持留学生的教学工作。感谢刘院长。

感谢国际教育学院办公室主任刘鲁吉博士。刘博士对待工作一向认真、周到、细致，是保证留学生教学工作正常运转不可或缺的助力。感谢刘博士。

感谢国际教育学院俄语教研室主任胡延新博士。胡博士也是一向工作认真，待人诚恳。我们两个人在工作中经常互相切磋、共同探讨。当然，主要是我向她请教和学习。感谢胡博士。

感谢侯春菊老师。侯老师在处理办公室日常教学事务的同时，还承担着留学生的汉语教学任务。对待汉语教学工作，侯老师很用心、很热情、很投入，也很有自己的思路、想法和见地，并拥有一批忠实的粉丝，甚至有的美国学生点名要上侯老师的课。感谢侯老师。

感谢王萌老师。王萌老师一直是英语教学的主力。除了认真完成自己承担的雅思课程教学工作之外，对于其他一些与英语教学有关的教研工作，王老师也一向是主动参与，积极承担，不辞辛苦，不计报酬。感谢王萌老师。

感谢王伟老师。王伟老师身为国际教育学院的团支部书记，在从事繁忙的学生日常管理工作之余，还承担了中国学生的剑桥英语课程的教学工作。不论是对待管理工作，还是教学工作，王老师都很用心、很认真、很细致、很尽责。感谢王伟老师。

还有王耀斌老师，王宗涛老师，殷源老师，国娇老师，马柳欣慰老师，李红星老师，娄耸老师，吴媛媛老师，王晓晴老师……感谢大家在工作中的相互合作与相互支持！由于篇幅所限，在此不再一一陈述大家的优长。

祝愿国际教育学院蓬勃发展，欣欣向荣！

最后，还要感谢中国民主促进会山东交通学院支部主委原所佳先生和所有的支部成员们，感谢大家给予我的关爱和支持！

李淑霞

2018 年 11 月 13 日